Wild!
Weird!
Wonderful!

MAINE.

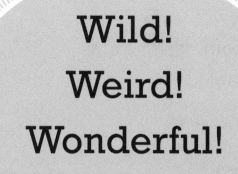

Wild!
Weird!
Wonderful!
MAINE.

BY EARL BRECHLIN

ISLANDPORT PRESS

ISLANDPORT PRESS

Islandport Press
P.O. Box 10
Yarmouth, Maine 04096
www.islandportpress.com
info@islandportpress.com

ISBN: 978-1-944762-80-3
Library of Congress Card Number: 2019931598
Printed in USA

Dean L. Lunt, Publisher
Teresa Lagrange, Book design

On the cover: Clockwise from left, Admiral Robert Peary in Arctic gear (*Courtesy of Wikicommons*); UFO over the Allagash (*Courtesy of ThinkStock*); British fleet destroying the Penobscot Expedition in 1779 (*Courtesy of National Maritime Museum in London*); and vintage postcard of Portland Observatory (*From Author's Collection*).

Back cover, top to bottom: giant octopus attacks a ship (*Courtesy of Wikicommons*); Moxie soda bottle; and fanciful depictions of the Meddybemps Howler (*Courtesy of Wikicommons*).

To all historians, private and professional, working alone or within groups and societies, and through libraries and educational institutions, to discover, uncover, rescue, protect, and preserve the artifacts, stories, and traditions of this incredible state. Thanks to you, the people of this time—and those in the future—will truly know the heart and soul of Maine.

Engraving of sawmill on the Penobscot at Old Town.
Courtesy of Digicommons.

Author's Note

So, you think you know Maine? Think again!

The Pine Tree State is not just a sprawling playground of woods, waters, mountains, rocky shores, quaint villages, hardy mill towns, lobsters, and lighthouses—as often portrayed in tourist brochures.

From Kittery to Fort Kent, from Calais to Camden, from Rangeley to Roque Bluffs, and from Bethel to Bucksport, Maine is filled with natural and human-made wonders. It has been, and is, home to quirky characters, remarkable inventors, historical firsts, ghosts, legends, landmarks, fairs, festivals, and culinary delights all born in the triumph of an indomitable spirit that has only grown during the past two centuries of statehood. *Wild! Weird! Wonderful! Maine.* is a celebration of all that makes the state unique, including people, places, and things both real and imagined.

The subjects in this book are a cross between affectionate history, a homespun version of *Ripley's Believe It or Not!*, and a collection of myths, legends, and truths shared for decades around hearths, campfires, and potbelly stoves.

No one place, no one person, no single historical event or ideology characterizes Maine. Rather, its truth is a marvelous amalgam realized over multiple generations of shared hardships and joys. Maine features an unapologetic climate, inspiring geography, hardscrabble economics, and a taciturn, yet open-minded culture. The relative strength and proportion of those factors ultimately determines what is or isn't authentic Maine.

Along with celebrating the Maine mystique, we hopefully will inspire you to explore for yourself all the things that define this fabulous state. What is it that makes Maine special? Close your eyes. Flip open this book, put your finger on a page—and just go!

We hope you will agree that *Wild! Weird! Wonderful!* is not just a fun and interesting read, but also a humble, yet comprehensive anthology of all things cool, quirky—and maybe just a little bit bizarre—about the Great State of Maine.

Helpful Hints and Advice

Along with celebrating the amazing scope and depth of Maine's history and culture, the aim of *Wild! Weird! Wonderful! Maine.* is designed to inspire folks to head out and explore places and attend events.

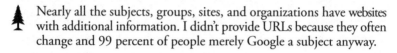 Nearly all the subjects, groups, sites, and organizations have websites with additional information. I didn't provide URLs because they often change and 99 percent of people merely Google a subject anyway.

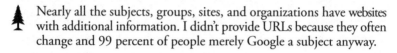 While I provided GPS coordinates for some backcountry locations, most places are easily accessible along public roads or streets. However, don't rely on just a cellphone map app as they seldom show enough detail to be useful.

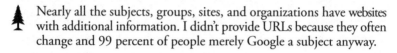 It goes without saying that you must make sure your vehicle, skill set, and physical condition are properly matched with the effort required to visit any backcountry location.

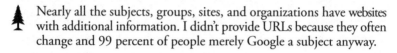 Please follow the Leave No Trace principle of "Take nothing but photographs, leave nothing but footprints."

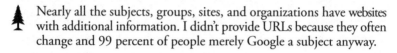 Because no one should be off on an adventure in Maine without a copy of DeLorme's *Maine Atlas and Gazetteer*, I provide the atlas grid coordinates for every place featured. In the atlas, each map page is numbered and includes a grid to help locate a specific area. For example, M36, C-2 means you will find the place on Map 36, within grid C-2.

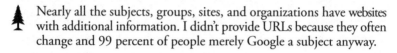 In the case of paper company, blueberry company, railroad rights of way, or conservation easement lands, please research and respect their rules governing access and safety.

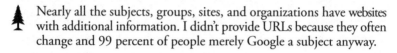 Acadia National Park, state parks, and other areas often charge entrance fees.

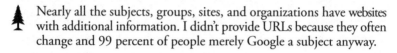 Please don't trespass on private property. Whenever in doubt, get permission.

Contents

A Brief Maine Primer

The Name "Maine"

While some historians have attempted to tie the name of Maine, the state, with a province of the same name in France, historian Charles Clark in *Maine, A History*, believes the term is entirely North American in origin. The area now known as Maine was first described in 1622 as the "Province of Maine."

" . . . These island-studded waters were customarily called 'the main,' spelled alternately maine, maigne, mayn, mayne, and even meign," Clark writes.

Other proposed names were strongly disliked by King Charles. The Maine State Library reports that he responded in a 1639 charter that it "shall forever hereafter be called and named the Province or County of Mayne and not by any other name or names whatsoever."

Prior to statehood (Maine split off from Massachusetts in 1820), some suggested the name Ligonia or Columbia, but Maine ultimately prevailed.

Place Names

Maine is home to a marvelous diversity of place names. Although, in a state with thousands of lakes, streams, and mountains it is also no surprise that many places have the same name.

The most popular is Mud Pond. There are sixty-five scattered about a state that is actually best known for its sparkling clear water.

There are forty-six Long Ponds, thirty-seven Bog Brooks, and nineteen Bald Mountains. Someone apparently found the time to name twenty-one Lost Ponds and there are fourteen Bar Islands.

In Maine, the terms lake and pond are used interchangeably. Ponds are sometimes much larger than nearby water bodies referred to as lakes.

Great ponds are any containment more than ten acres in size. These are controlled by the state, even when surrounded by private land. Landowners cannot block foot access to great ponds.

Many places with Native American names can be difficult to pronounce. Try saying Mooselookmeguntic Lake (Moose-look-meah-gun-tic) real fast. Many people stumble over Nesowadnehunk Lake (Sow-deh-hunk). When in doubt, ask. Most folks are happy to help.

Place Numbers

You may not be at the end of the world, but you might be able to see it from a place where geographers run out of names and resort to numbers.

Wilderness areas are broken down into townships (T) and ranges (R). Hence designations such as T2-R11. Some explorers will encounter brightly painted posts with the letters and numbers at key road and river crossings and at township line junctions. They are useful for navigation purposes in areas with few landmarks.

The letters WELS are added to some townships and stand for West of the East Line Survey or West of the Easterly Line of the State. Other groups of letters are used to help reduce confusion over townships of similar number.

Perhaps the most interesting "slice" of land in Maine is famed Misery Gore. Gores are unusual triangular or rectangular areas of land that suddenly appeared when various survey results didn't jibe. They are sort of the surveyor's equivalent of not being able to balance a checkbook. Most have been absorbed into nearby townships over the years.

Misery Gore, is a long narrow strip with an end on the west shore of Moosehead Lake. It is a half-mile wide at one end and tapers to a sharp point more than twenty miles to the west. Another fabled gore is Coburn Gore, an irregular piece of land formed by the circuitous boundary with Canada in Western Maine.

Maine By The Numbers

Counties (16)	Androscoggin, Aroostook, Cumberland, Franklin, Hancock, Kennebec, Knox, Lincoln, Oxford, Penobscot, Piscataquis, Sagadahoc, Somerset, Waldo, Washington, and York
Land Area	30,843 square miles
Length of Coastline	3,500 miles
Lakes and Ponds	6,000
Forest	17 million acres
Persons per Square Mile	43.1
Largest City	Portland
Capital	Augusta
Statehood	Became the 23rd on March 15, 1820
Population	Approximately 1.34 million

Flag

The coat of arms of Maine is placed on a blue field of the same shade of blue in the flag of the United States. Adopted by the Legislature of 1909.

Maine State Seal

The State of Maine seal is a shield in silver. It features a pine tree with a moose lying at the foot of it. On the left side of the shield is a farmer resting on a scythe and on the right side is a seaman resting on an anchor. The whole is surrounded by a crest and topped by the North Star with the word Dirigo, meaning "I lead."

Stuff O' Maine

Every state has its list of official mascots, symbols often hammered out in long and hard legislative debates. Here's the latest list from Maine.

Animal	Moose
Ballad	Ballad of the 20th Maine
Berry	Blueberry
Beverage	Moxie
Bird	Black-capped Chickadee
Cat	Maine Coon Cat
Crustacean	Lobster
Dessert	Blueberry pie
Fish	Landlocked salmon
Flag	Flag of Maine
Flower	White Pine Cone and Tassel
Fossil	Pertica quadrifaria (fern)
Gemstone	Tourmaline
Herb	Wintergreen
Insect	Honeybee
Motto	Dirigo (I Lead)
Nickname	The Pine Tree State
Soil	Chesuncook (soil)
Song	"State of Maine Song" by Roger Vinton Snow
Treat	Whoopie pie
Tree	Eastern White Pine
Vessel	Schooner *Bowdoin*

Maine Claims to Fame (alphabetically)

Abbott	Maine's "First Town"
Aroostook County	Agricultural Capital
Belfast	Broiler (Chicken) Capital
Bethel	Nordic Ski Capital
Boothbay	Boating Capital
Brooklin	Boat Building Capital
Camden	Tall Ship Capital
Cherryfield	Wild Blueberry Capital
Clinton	Dairy Capital
Eastport	Sardine Capital
Farmington	Earmuff Capital
Franklin	Granite Capital
Greenville	Snowmobiling Capital
Guilford	Lilac Capital
Norway	Snowshoe Capital
Portland	Maine's Culinary Capital
Rockland	Art Capital
Scarborough	Digital Capital
Seal Cove	Trail Sign Capital
Searsport	Antique Capital (contested by Wells)
South Paris	Gemstone Capital
Stockton Springs	Clam Capital
Stonington	Lobster Capital
Strong	Toothpick Capital
Waldoboro	Home of the Five-Masted Schooner
West Paris	Clothespin Capital

Mount Katahdin
Courtesy of Wikicommons.

Maine's Tallest Mountain Peaks

Maine, Vermont and New Hampshire are the only states in New England with mountains with peaks of more than 4,000 feet. Hikers who have reached the top of them all, some 67 in total, can apply to become members of the Appalachian Mountain Club's 4,000-Footer Club.

Peak	Elevation in Feet
1. Baxter Peak, Katahdin	5,267
2. Hamlin Peak, Baxter State Park	4,756
3. Sugarloaf	4,237
4. Crocker Mountain	4,228
5. Old Speck	4,170
6. North Brother, Baxter State Park	4,151
7. Bigelow, West Peak	4,145
8. Saddleback Mountain	4,116
9. Bigelow, Avery Peak	4,090
10. South Crocker Mountain	4,052
11. Mount Abraham	4,049
12. Saddleback Horn	4,023
13. Mount Redington	4,010
14. Spaulding Mountain	4,007

Maine's Largest Lakes

By any measure, Maine has plenty of large lakes. While some may be longer, or deeper, here is the list of the ten largest tabulated by surface area. In many cases, the final body of water resulted from construction of dams that flooded multiple smaller lakes (noted).

Name	Square Miles
1. Moosehead Lake	117
2. Sebago Lake	45
3. Chesuncook Lake[1]	36
4. Flagstaff Lake	31
5. Twin Lake System[2]	29
6. Spednic Lake	27
7. Mooselookmeguntic Lake[3]	26
8. East Grand Lake	24
9. West Grand Lake	23.5
10. Chamberlain Lake	17.5

[1] Includes Caribou Lake
[2] Includes So. & No. Twin Lakes, Pemadumcook and Ambajejus
[3] Includes Cupsuptic

A quiet cove on Students Island in the Stephen Phillips Preserve in Mooselookmeguntic Lake. *From Author's Collection.*

Maine's Longest Rivers

Maine has more than 70 rivers and streams of more than 20 miles in length. Below is a list of the 25 longest including various branches.

Name	Length in Miles
Saint John River	331
Penobscot River	240
Androscoggin River	174
Kennebec River	170
Saco River	121
Aroostook River	100
Mattawamkeag River	83
Dead River (with South Branch)	74
Sebasticook River	72
Allagash River	69
Dead River (with North Branch)	67
Piscataquis River	67
Sandy River	65
Moose River	65
Fish River	62
Sheepscot River	55
Narraguagus River	48
Baskahegan Stream	48
Magalloway River	48
Little Androscoggin River	47
Machias River	46
Big Black River	45
Passadumkeag River	45
Carrabassett River	43
Pleasant River	43

The deep, cool rocks along this stretch of the Saco River in Hollis where Native Americans used to store food in summer gave the scenic canyon its name.
From Author's Collection.

Western Mountains

Western Mountains

From Augusta and Lewiston on the more gentle terrain of the east, to the Rangeley Lakes and ski areas such as Sugarloaf and Sunday River, the Western Mountains region is home to spectacular landscapes as well as friendly towns and villages nestled where fertile soil attracted early settlers and entrepreneurs seeking to harness the rushing waters of local rivers for industry and transportation.

Here you'll find an annual festival dedicated to the unique taste of Moxie, as well as the Appalachian Trail's toughest mile in Mahoosuc Notch. Savor the view from Height of Land along Route 17 as you approach Rangeley, knowing this scenery also attracted cult figure Wilhelm Reich and his controversial Orgone research experiments.

Fun, of course, has always been a high priority in this part of Maine; so check out the world's tallest snowman in Bethel or consider entering the annual North American Wife Carrying Championships where first prize is not only cash, but the wife's weight in Oktoberfest beer.

High tech and low tech live hand-in-hand here. While Bryant Pond was the nation's last town to still operate hand-cranked telephones, Andover includes Telstar, the US ground station constructed to send and receive signals from the first live television satellite beamed across the Atlantic.

Maine is seldom a place people associate with geological riches; it is famous, however, for its spectacular tourmaline used in jewelry, as well as being the place where the world-renowned "Bumpus Beryl," an enormous two-ton crystal, was discovered in 1928. While you may not want to spend an afternoon mining for gems (although you can), one thing is certain; there's plenty of great Maine history and natural wonders to discover in the Western Mountains.

Opposite (clockwise from top): A vintage postcard view of the Moxie Horse Car (*Author's Collection*); an early postcard image showing the Poland Spring House (*From Author's Collection*); picture on the Vicki Van Meter Memorial in Augusta (*Courtesy Van Meter Family*); and Cascade Stream Gorge at Rangeley (*Courtesy of Kurt Peterson*).

Town Abandons 'Crank' Calls For Dial

The cozy village of Bryant Pond in Woodstock was the last place in America to give up hand-cranked telephones. In October 1983, the tiny local telephone company's 431 crank callers entered the modern era, finally abandoning equipment installed in the 1930s. The move was fiercely protested by a group called "Don't Yank the Crank." Hand-cranked phones required the user to vigorously rotate a crank that drove a magneto that signaled the operator you wanted to make a call.

This giant telephone monument commemorates Bryant Pond as the last place in the United States to use hand-cranked phones. *Courtesy of Woodstock Historical Society.*

Some twenty-five years later in 2008, a 14-foot high metal statue of a candlestick phone was installed in Remembrance Park on Main Street in honor of that fateful day. The iron sculpture by Gil Whitman is considered to be the largest of its kind in the world and weighs more than a ton.

A few hundred yards away from the telephone monument is the giant clothespin sign, the largest of its type in the world, that advertised the Lewis Mann and Son factory in town. *Maine Atlas: M10, B5*

First Fisherman Ike Liked Rangeley

Although Herbert Hoover and Teddy Roosevelt are among those who wetted a line near Rangeley, the most memorable presidential visit was likely that of President Dwight D. Eisenhower, who spent time at local sporting camps and fished the lakes and streams in 1955.

Far from a solitary experience, Ike was accompanied by a swarm of Secret Service agents and more than seventy reporters. Legend holds that Ike had nary a nibble the first day. That evening his guide called other guides and friends and asked them to catch as many big fish as possible and "salt" the pool at Little Boy Falls on the nearby

Magalloway River. The next morning at breakfast the guide casually suggested the president try that spot. Ike hooked three impressive fish, including a twenty-three-inch salmon, right in front of the news cameras.

Other reports claim game wardens also assisted in the escapade.

Either way, Eisenhower enjoyed Maine much better than Vermont where he was skunked. In 1970, the Maine Federation of Republican Women placed a bronze plaque on rocks at the pool. Eisenhower, a talented oil painter, even did a portrait of his friend and guide Don Cameron. *Maine Atlas: M28, B1*

President Dwight "Ike" Eisenhower (left) fishing at Little Boy Falls near Rangeley.
Courtesy of Outdoor Heritage Museum.

Hiker on Mahoosuc Notch.
Courtesy of Wikicommons.

Wild!

Mahoosuc Notch: AT's Toughest Mile

The renowned Appalachian Trail, or AT, runs more than 2,200 miles from Georgia to Maine and has no shortage of candidates for hardest mile. Still, a single stretch in the Western Mountains of Maine, not far from Bethel, is the undisputed king. Mahoosuc Notch is a deep, mile-long scramble over and under a pile of house-sized boulders that

Bumpus Beryl Sets World Record

Western Maine is famous for its semiprecious stones such as tourmaline and topaz, but one discovery set a world record.

At the Bumpus Quarry in a former potato field in Albany Township near Bethel, the largest single crystal of beryl was discovered by Harry Bumpus while mining feldspar in 1928. Aquamarine and emerald are examples of beryl.

More like a colossal, hexagonal log of crystal, the largest specimen was twenty-seven-feet long and weighed an amazing 52,000 pounds. A blend of aqua and golden colors, it tapered from four feet to nine inches in diameter. It had to be extracted in sections.

Several masses of rose quartz six to eight feet across were also uncovered at the same time. Pieces of the Bumpus Beryl were shipped to the American Museum of Natural History in New York and the Harvard Museum of Natural History in Cambridge, Massachusetts.

The largest remaining piece of the Bumpus Beryl, weighing more than two tons, was returned to Maine in 2017 and placed on display at the Maine Mineral and Gem Museum in Bethel. *Maine Atlas: M10, C3*

is not for the faint of heart. Barely thirty yards wide at the base, the notch is sandwiched between four-hundred-foot granite cliffs. Sunlight rarely touches its depths and ice can remain deep underground long into summer. While passing through boulder caves, hikers can frequently hear the sound of an underground stream even deeper.

Hikers frequently are forced to remove their packs to fit through narrow openings in the abrasive rocks. For many years the forlorn skeleton of a moose, which had become trapped in the notch, was visible along the trail.

Heading northbound on the AT, the path drops more than a one thousand feet from Fulling Mill Mountain. The trail through the notch gradually ascends to the east before turning north and going 1,400 feet nearly straight up the side of Mahoosuc Arm. *Maine Atlas: M18, E1*

Lock is Reminder of Long-lost Canal

Maine endeavored to begin its own "Big Dig," long before anyone thought of rerouting highways under Boston. Just after Maine became a state in 1820, business leaders decided to act on their dream of creating a quick and easy way to move goods from Portland to the interior of Western Maine. The idea for the Cumberland and Oxford (C&O) Canal was born.

The waterway stretched forty miles inland through Sebago Lake to Long Lake in Bridgton. It took nearly five years to dig the thirty-foot-wide canal by hand. When heading upstream, a canal boat had to pass through twenty-seven locks with a total elevation gain of 280 feet. Barge crews used sails on the lakes and horses attached to tow ropes in canal sections.

Competition from railroads which could operate when the canal was iced over, spelled doom for profitability and the C&O closed after thirty years. The bank chartered to help fund it, Canal Bank, continued on for more than a century and a half. Only the Songo Lock, between Brandy Pond and Sebago Lake, remains in use and nearly five thousand pleasure boats use it annually. Located in Sebago Lake State Park, the lock is on the National Register of Historic Places.

For years the excursion boat *Songo River Queen II*, which operates out of Bridgton, made a passage through Songo Lock on some trips. However, the practice ended when the state replaced a swinging bridge upstream with an immovable design. *Maine Atlas: M5, B1*

Mainers Have Always Prized 'Moxie'

True Mainers are proud of their Moxie, both in their attitudes and in their fondness for a soft drink of that name.

In 1876, Dr. Augustin Thompson of Lowell, Massachusetts, a native of Union, Maine, created a concoction he named "Moxie Nerve Food." Although the formula, like that of Coca-Cola, which came along a decade later, is super secret, it reportedly contains gentian root.

Although an acquired taste, Moxie has won over a legion of fans, including President Calvin Coolidge, author E.B. White, and sports great Ted Williams. It was named the official soft drink of Maine in 2005.

Since 1982 the town of Lisbon has held an annual Moxie Festival featuring a parade, block party, and fireworks.

A thirty-three-foot-tall Moxie Bottle House rescued by members of the New England Moxie Congress was restored and put on display indoors at the Matthews Museum of Maine Heritage in Union, along with other displays of Moxie memorabilia and merchandise. Located on the

Vintage postcard showing Moxie Bottle House.
From Author's Collection.

Union Fairgrounds, the house is open in July and August.

Coca-Cola bought the Moxie brand in 2018, but the name continues to be associated with courage, daring, and spirit. *Maine Atlas: M14, D1*

Hermit Evaded Capture for Decades

Along with stealing items from homes and camps around North Pond in Smithfield, Christopher Knight, who would later be dubbed the North Pond Hermit, also seized the imaginations of people curious how he could survive alone in the woods for nearly thirty years.

After abandoning his car near Greenville, a then-20-year-old Knight made several attempts to live off the land, eventually settling in Smithfield. He situated his campsite in a cluster of large boulders where he set up tents and tarps. To survive, he stole food, clothing, propane canisters for heating and cooking, reading material, and other household goods from residences around the lake. Police estimate he committed more than one thousand thefts.

He was careful to walk on rocks to avoid leaving tracks and sometimes took canoes to ferry his loot back to camp. He rarely built a fire, kept his hair cut, and shaved regularly. He told authorities he'd wake before dawn on below-zero mornings and pace about his campsite to stay warm.

Knight was captured by Game Warden Sgt. Terry Hughes on April 4, 2013, while taking food from the kitchen at the Pine Tree Camp in Rome. He was sentenced to seven months in jail and ordered to pay $2,000 in restitution.

Knight's story was profiled in the book *Stranger in the Woods* by Michael Finkle. His former campsite is on private property closed to the public. *Maine Atlas: M20, D4*

Healing Waters Launch Spring to Fame

An inn owner's claim about the healing power of a local spring in 1844 launched a juggernaut that is today one of the largest water bottling companies in the world.

An early postcard image showing the Poland Spring House.
From Author's Collection.

Hiram Ricker's Mansion House grew in popularity, largely through his promotion of the restorative properties of the spring water. The property eventually exploded into the Poland Spring House resort in 1876, which neighbors nicknamed "Ricker's Folly."

The stately hotel on the site eventually expanded to include more than 350 guest rooms, a barbershop, bowling alley, and music hall. The family opened similar resorts including the Samoset in Rockport and Mt. Kineo House in Greenville. The Poland Spring House burned flat in 1975.

The Maine State Building from the 1893 Chicago World's Fair was purchased, moved and reassembled on the property as a library and art gallery.

The Rickers began selling Poland Spring Water around New England in 1859. Their company opened a modern bottling plant and graceful spring house on the property in 1907. It is now a museum.

The company was sold to Perrier in 1980. Perrier was acquired by Nestlé Waters North America in 1992. Poland Spring has grown over the years to include eight water sources around Maine and bottling plants that employ more than nine hundred people. It bottles approximately 950 million gallons annually. *Maine Atlas: M5, A3*

Mountain Home to Mattress Mayhem

In the annals of the "What can go wrong?" and "Hold my beer," halls of fame there should be a special place for the founders of one of New England's most wacky ski mountain activities—the Shawnee Peak Mattress Race.

Held each March, you can choose your division, including twin, full, queen or king—and register a two-to-four person team for the chance to ride that old twin-coil or innerspring to fame and infamy. Costumes and decorations are encouraged. If it's cold, don't forget an extra blanket.

Some racers have hit speeds of thirty miles per hour over the two-hundred-foot-long course, which in past years has included a small jump. The key, according to organizers, is wrapping the mattress in plastic to reduce friction. The winner gets—what else?—a new king-size mattress.

Helmets are mandatory and, for obvious reasons, waterbeds are banned. You'll need a lift ticket and there is a modest entry fee to help underwrite proper disposal of mattresses. The ski area is located off Route 302 in Bridgton. *Maine Atlas: M4, A3*

Santas Shred Slopes for Charity

What can be better than seeing Old St. Nick himself out on the ski slopes in Maine? How about more than 240 Santas on skis and snowboards . . . in one place . . . at one time?

Sunday River resort in Newry has been holding an annual "Santas Hit the Slopes for Cause" event each December for the last twenty years to benefit the nonprofit River Fund, which supports youth education and recreation initiatives. Each Santa pays $20 to buy a lift ticket for the Sunday event and for another day later in the month. In 2019, the event raised more than $6,200—a new record.

Each entrant is required to come up with their own Santa attire but it must include red coat, red pants, Santa hat, and a white beard.

All participants group together for the picturesque ride up the South Ridge chairlift before posing for a group photo and then descending on the Broadway Trail en masse. The event is held rain, snow, or shine. *Maine Atlas: M10, A2*

Samantha Smith Sows Seeds of Peace

Nixon went to China. Reagan urged Gorbachev to tear down the Berlin Wall, but it was Samantha Smith from Maine who helped establish a true détente with the people of the Soviet Union.

In 1982, the ten-year-old girl from Manchester wrote a personal letter to Soviet General Secretary Yuri Andropov. Her letter, urging peace, was published in *Pravda*, but Andropov did not respond. Pressing on, Smith wrote to the Russian UN ambassador, who nudged Andropov and the General Secretary invited her to visit. She accepted.

Smith instantly became America's best-known goodwill ambassador and was invited to participate in peace-making activities around the world. She appeared on numerous network news programs and spent two weeks in Russia as Andropov's guest, although due to his health, she never met him face to face.

The Samantha Smith statue located on the grounds of the State Capitol in Augusta. *From Author's Collection.*

Upon her return to Maine, Smith was welcomed with a red carpet, roses, and a limousine. Tragically, she and her father died in a Bar Harbor Airlines crash near the Lewiston-Auburn Airport on August 25, 1985. She was just 13.

A bronze statue in honor of Smith, dove in hand, was erected next to the Maine State Museum on the grounds of the State Capitol in Augusta in 1986. A foundation was also created in her memory. *Maine Atlas: M76, C3*

Lion's Roar Echoes Through History

An early steam locomotive currently on display at the Maine State Museum in Augusta, played a major role in powering the state's logging industry.

Christened the *Lion*, the bright green, nine-ton steam engine was built in 1846 by Hinkley Drury Locomotive Works in Boston and shipped to Machias by sea. Rated for 100 horsepower, it began service on the Whitneyville and Machiasport Railroad, Maine's second oldest, hauling timber from mills to tidewater wharves. In a cloud of billowing smoke and swirling steam it ran atop iron straps affixed to wooden rails. Its top speed was around ten miles per hour.

A round trip between the railroad's namesake towns covered about sixteen miles. During that trip the *Lion* would consume six hundred gallons of water and about half a cord of firewood. Later that year, the *Lion* was joined in service by a sister engine, the *Tiger*.

After forty-five years of service both locomotives were sold to a man in Portland. The *Tiger* saw service at a paper mill and its fate is uncertain.

The *Lion* remained on display in Portland until 1905 when it was given to the University of Maine at Machias. In 1976, it was placed on the National Register of Historic Places as the oldest American-built locomotive in New England.

The *Lion* was donated to the state museum in 1985. *Maine Atlas: M76, C3*

Telstar Station Enabled Transatlantic Television

While many people view Maine as a place steeped in old traditions, in the early 1960s it was at the tip of the telecommunications technological spear.

The era of live, transatlantic broadcasts of television signals was inaugurated at the Telstar Ground Receiving Station in Andover. The first black-and-white image to be beamed from North America to

Europe was a waving American flag in front of the facility sent on July 11, 1962. That same day, the first long-distance telephone call by satellite was made by then Vice President Lyndon Johnson who spoke to AT&T Chairman Fred Kappel who was in Andover.

The distinctive dome of the Telstar ground station in Andover as it looms over a nearby road. *Courtesy of Wikicommons.*

Less than two weeks later, the first public live television broadcast between the continents was shared via Telstar. That all was made possible by the launch of the 171-pound Telstar 1 satellite from Cape Canaveral in Florida on July 10, 1962.

Andover was chosen as one of several receiving stations around the world due to its location in a mountain valley that shielded the antennas from interference.

The main antenna, some seven-stories high and weighing 340 tons, was located in a 160-foot diameter inflatable bubble. The complex was torn down in the 1990s. A plaque commemorating its achievements is located on the Andover Village Green.

Telstar 1, which was damaged by a US government high-altitude nuclear weapon test, remained in service for only seven months, although it is still in orbit. There are now more than 260 communications satellites circling the Earth. *Maine Atlas: M18, D3*

Rock, Mineral Display is Out-Of-This-World

With the goal of showcasing Maine's varied and proud geological history, the Maine Mineral and Gem Museum in Bethel offers displays of unique and interesting rocks, minerals, and gems, including the renowned Perham Collection, which was once housed in a local rock shop that attracted collectors for nearly a century. It was founded by master miner Frank Perham.

In 2017, the museum acquired one of the last remaining segments of the largest beryl crystal ever found on Earth, the Bumpus Beryl,

Giant Snowpeople Set Guinness Records

Imagine making snowmen and snowwomen so big you must import tons of the white stuff from miles around and use heavy equipment to complete the project.

That's exactly what happened in Bethel in 1999 and again in 2008 when people built snowpeople so large they made the Guinness Book of World Records.

Standing some 113 feet high, Angus, King of the Mountain, a nod to Maine's former governor and current US Sen. Angus King, required an estimated eight

million pounds of snow. Tires were used for eyes, twenty-five-foot-tall spruce trees for arms, and Telstar Middle School kids created a twenty-foot in diameter fleece hat. Built in February, it didn't fully melt until June.

In 2008, Bethel again rallied to the cause, eclipsing its own previous creation by twenty feet for a total height of 133 feet making the world's tallest snowman a snowwoman. Total weight of Olympia, an homage to Maine's US Sen. Olympia Snowe, was an estimated thirteen million pounds. Some two thousand feet of rope was used for her hair.

Both sculptures, which towered more than ten stories tall over nearby homes, took more than a month to build.

Maine Atlas: M10, B3

A giant snowwoman in Bethel.
Courtesy of Bethel Area Chamber of Commerce.

which was uncovered in a quarry just a few miles down the road. It had been on display at the American Museum of Natural History in New York.

The museum also has one of the world's best displayed collections of extraterrestrial rocks, including meteorites that originated on Mars, the Moon, and the Asteroid Belt. Some of the interplanetary fragments are more than 4.5 billion years old.

The museum is located at 99 Main Street in Bethel and is open six days a week (Closed Tuesdays). *Maine Atlas: M10, B3*

Preserve is 'Secret' Wilderness Playground

The Stephen Phillips Preserve, which covers six thousand acres around Mooselookmeguntic Lake and on its islands, is a true hidden wilderness recreation gem and one of the largest in Maine.

A board of trustees watches over this gift from Stephen Phillips, of Salem, Massachusetts, who began acquiring land in the early 1960s.

The preserve, which operates out of a modest log cabin on Stephens Road, protects four miles of shoreline and has more than sixty campsites that can be reserved in advance. Some are located on the mainland and can be accessed by a short trail walk. Others are only accessible by boat. All feature fire pits, picnic tables and access to an outhouse. Jugs of water, firewood, and canoe rentals are available at the preserve office.

Some of the campsites on Students Island, site of the former Birches lodge and sporting camps, have their own beach access depending on water levels. There are hiking trails on the island, while the swimming and fishing is always fabulous.

There is a website where you can view a campsite and even see pictures of each site. However, you'll have to make reservations the old-fashioned way, by mail or by phone, once the office opens and the line is reconnected each May. *Maine Atlas: M18, A3*

Win Your Wife's Weight in Beer

Bragging rights and the chance to win cash and your wife's weight in beer is more than enough to attract hundreds of competitors to the annual North American Wife Carrying Championship at Sunday River in Newry each October.

For more than twenty years husbands have been tossing the metaphorical "old ball and chain" over their shoulders for the 278-yard dash through an obstacle course that features an uphill track, log barriers, and a mud pit dubbed "The Widow Maker." Over time, competitors have honed their technique, with the most popular having the wife riding head down, legs over the husband's shoulders, and arms clutched tightly around his chest.

Contestants in the annual North American Wife Carrying Championships at Sunday River in Newry. *Courtesy of Sunday River Ski Resort.*

Being a spectator is free although each couple who wants to race must pay $50. It's a popular competition and the field is limited so there's often a wait list.

The winner, determined by final runoff, not just overall time, receives the wife's weight in Goose Island Oktoberfest beer, five times her weight in cash, and is entered into the World Championship in Finland. *Maine Atlas: M10, A2*

Hilltop Castle Home to Sex Scientist

One of the most enigmatic and controversial figures of the early twentieth century, Wilhelm Reich, was a doctor and psychoanalyst who sought to educate the world about the mysterious properties of

"Orgones" a biological energy he claimed was related to sexuality and health. Reich was considered by some a mad scientist and coined the term "sexual revolution." He built his stone castle observatory "Orgonon" on a hill just outside Rangeley in 1948, where he continued his experiments by building Orgone Accumulators, some of which were large enough for a person to sit inside.

During his career, Reich was a colleague of Sigmund Freud and conducted a joint experiment with Albert Einstein.

He also invented gigantic truck-mounted "Cloudbuster" devices he claimed could generate rain in even the driest climates. In 1951, Maine blueberry farmers paid him after he deployed the device to their fields and it rained later that evening.

Reich's writings and experiments earned him powerful critics. The Food and Drug Administration banned the interstate sale of his devices and literature in 1947. Tons of his pamphlets and books were burned in New York City. In 1956, Reich was convicted of violating the ban and sent to jail. He died of a heart attack in prison just days before his scheduled release.

Orgonon, on Dodge Pond Road, is open to the public seasonally and a former cottage where Reich lived on the property is available for rent. *Maine Atlas: M28, E4*

Orgonon, the Rangeley home of scientist and sex researcher Wilhelm Reich (inset). *From Author's Collection.*

Mount Mica is Maine Motherlode

Maine has a long history with its Official State Gem, tourmaline. The first discoveries were made around the time Maine became a state in 1820. In October, Elijah Hamlin and Ezekiel Holmes were exploring the hills near their homes when a flash of green light from the roots of an overturned tree caught their eye. They discovered more the following spring. (Hamlin's younger brother, Hannibal, went on to be vice president during Abraham Lincoln's first term.)

Mount Mica went on to become one of the premier mineral locations in the country with both green and unusual pink "watermelon" crystals being recovered.

According to the Smithsonian Museum of Natural History, one of, if not the, largest specimen, nearly thirteen inches long, was found in 1972 at the Plumbago Mine in Newry. It earned the nickname "Jolly Green Giant."

It was discovered by miners tunneling and blasting open pockets of tourmaline in which they recovered "bushel baskets" of crystals.

The tunnels were collapsed for safety reasons in 1974. In 2009, rare blue tourmaline was found in the Plumbago Mine. A large blue crystal dubbed "The President," was turned into several gems including one presented to President Barack Obama on his visit to Maine in 2010. *Maine Atlas: M11, C2*

World is Your Oyster in Lynchville

The entire world is just a few miles away when you stand in front of the World Traveler signpost in Lynchville in Albany Township, near Bethel. Of course, the distances aren't to countries and cities, but rather to Maine towns named for other nations.

Erected in the 1930s to promote tourism, the sign stands at the intersection of Routes 5 and 35. It instantly became one of the most popular postcard subjects in the state.

The towns/international place names include Norway, Paris, Denmark, Naples, Sweden, Poland, Mexico, Peru, and China. Why more similar-named towns weren't included, such as Moscow, Belfast, Lisbon, Rome, and Vienna, to name a few, isn't exactly clear.

Originally constructed of wood, it now incorporates steel to reduce chance of theft and vandalism, which has occurred in the past. Over the years, all segments of the sign have been replaced or repaired.

While many of the towns were originally named for countries, Norway is an exception. The town's name is actually a typo. When it was incorporated as part of Massachusetts in 1797, the desired name was either Norwich or Norage. The

This signpost in Lynchville, near Bethel, encourages travelers to visit the world—all without leaving the great State of Maine.
Courtesy of Wikicommons.

name on the papers, however, was recorded as Norway, and it stuck. The sign is on private property, but photography is allowed. *Maine Atlas: M10, D3*

Augusta

Augusta Is True Heart of Maine

It took seven years after Maine became a state in 1820 for Augusta to become its capital. Portland served as the first capital and wanted to keep that honor permanently. Other towns vying for capital status included Waterville, Wiscasset, Brunswick, Hallowell, and Belfast. However, Augusta, located between Portland and Bangor, won out.

Located at the head of navigable water on the mighty Kennebec River, Augusta was inhabited by Native Americans for centuries. It first served as a trading post for the Pilgrims and other early colonists.

Now a center of business and commerce, in addition to government, Augusta is the eastern most state capital in the United States. The community is also home to numerous veteran cemeteries and memorials, as well as the Veterans Administration state headquarters and Togus Medical Center.

Maine State House

The Maine State House, erected at the corner of State and Capitol streets, opened in 1832. Charles Bulfinch, who designed the Massachusetts State House, as well as the US Capitol, was the architect. Oxen hauled granite from quarries in nearby Hallowell for the project. The building has been added to and remodeled multiple times over the last nearly two hundred years. The statue of Minerva atop the copper dome is covered with gold leaf. A stainless-steel time capsule was buried in front of the building in 1989. It is slated to be opened in 2029. *Maine Atlas: M76, C3*

Hall of Flags

The Hall of Flags in Maine's State House was created after the Civil War to honor the more than 80,000 men who served in the Union Army and Navy. Nearly 8,500 were killed in battle or died of disease. Several captured Confederate battle flags were returned in the 1930s. Over the years, flags that have seen service in World War I, World War II, and the Korean War have been added. *Maine Atlas: M76, C3*

Opposite (clockwise from top): Old Fort Western; Maine Civilian Conservation Corps Monument near the Maine State Library; and the Blaine House. *From Author's Collection.*

Fort Western

Built in 1754 by the British during the French and Indian War, Augusta's Fort Western served as a trading post. It was never attacked directly. Listed on the National Register of Historic Places, it is the oldest log fort in the United States. Named for Thomas Western, a friend of a colonial governor, the outpost played host to Benedict Arnold during his ill-fated expedition to attack Quebec in 1775.

Maine Atlas: M76, B3

Police/Fire/EMS Memorials

Maine's official Law Enforcement, Firefighter, and EMS memorials are located in Memorial Park on the grounds of the State House Complex on State Street. The Law Enforcement Memorial contains the names of eighty-six public servants killed in the line of duty: the first, Ebenezer Parker of Cumberland in 1808, and the most recent, Deputy Eugene Cole of the Somerset Sheriff's Department in 2018.

The Firefighters Memorial is centered around a distinctive black granite silhouette of a firefighter. Individual names are kept on plaques used in a traveling exhibition. Maine's EMS personnel are honored a few yards away with a memorial featuring multiple granite obelisks, one with a list of eight names of those who died in the line of duty.

Maine Atlas: M76, C3

The Blaine House

Located a stone's throw from the State House, the Blaine House on State Street is the official residence of Maine's governor. It was built in 1833, and purchased three decades later by Maine's Speaker of the House, James G. Blaine. Blaine also served in the US House, including as speaker, in the US Senate, and as US Secretary of State. He ran for president against Grover Cleveland, and narrowly lost, in 1884.

The House was donated to the state for use by the governor in 1919.

Maine Atlas: M76, C3

Guy Gannett House

Built in 1911 for Maine newspaper publishing magnate Guy P. Gannett, (no connection to today's media giant Gannett) this house on State Street in Augusta was a home of the future—sporting full electric lighting and a central vacuuming system. It is currently being developed as Maine's First Amendment Museum. Including in Gannett's holdings were the *Portland Press Herald, Kennebec Journal,* and *Waterville Morning Sentinel.*

Maine Atlas: M76, C3

Maine Civilian Conservation Corps Memorial

During the Great Depression, the Civilian Conservation Corps put more than three million young people to work on public infrastructure projects. There were more than two-dozen camps in Maine, including at Acadia National Park and Baxter State Park. In all, more than 16,700 Mainers served, along with 1,600 staff and supervisors. They helped create the recreational infrastructure enjoyed by millions to this day. The memorial to their labors is just outside the Maine State Museum on the State House complex grounds.

Maine Atlas: M76, C3

Youngest Pilot Statue

Vicki Van Meter was only 11 years old when she (and an instructor) set out from the Augusta Airport to fly to San Diego, California, in just five days—making her one of the youngest transcontinental pilots ever. A year later, she became the youngest ever to fly solo across the Atlantic Ocean. A statue in her honor was installed in the lobby of the airport in 2010.

Maine Atlas: M76, B2

Rangeley

Carrie Stevens Monument

Carrie Gertrude Stevens was an avid fly fisher and fly maker. Among her most famous was the Grey Ghost Streamer. During the 1930s, sportsmen estimate nearly half of the record fish taken at Upper Dam were caught on a fly she tied. She tied flies without fancy equipment and sold them at her home near Upper Dam to passing fishermen. A monument at Upper Dam commemorates her importance to the sport. *Maine Atlas: M28, E3*

Middle Dam

This circa 1850s cribwork dam, originally built to help facilitate log drives, has been rebuilt and raised numerous times over its 170-year life. A major upgrade is also planned for 2020. Holding back the waters of Richardson Lake, the dam is the official start point for the Rapid River, renowned for its spectacular trout fishing. The large wooden structure that covered the dam offered protection from the weather for the mechanisms that raised the gates to release water. *Maine Atlas: M18, B1*

Louise Dickinson Rich

Living in a cabin on the Rapid River near Middle Dam, Louise Dickinson Rich penned *We Took to the Woods* in 1942, chronicling life in the remote Maine woods. The couple actually lived in two adjacent homes, a larger, more open one in summer, and a cozy cabin, just a few feet away, in winter. Other works included *Happy the Land* and *Innocence Under the Elms*. *Maine Atlas: M18, B1*

Cascade Stream Gorge

Noted photographers have flocked from around New England for more than one hundred years to get images of the cascades in the ninety-foot deep Cascade Stream Gorge, just off Route 4. The fifty-acre preserve with moderate hiking trail is on the Maine Register of Critical Areas. *Maine Atlas: M28, E5*

Opposite (clockwise from top): A vintage postcard image of Middle Dam in the Rangeley Region (*From Author's Collection*); Maine writer Louise Dickinson Rich (*Courtesy of Outdoor Heritage Museum*); and a hand-crafted Rangeley boat (*From Author's Collection*).

A view looking out over Mooselookmeguntic Lake from the Height of Land along Route 17. *Courtesy of Digicommons.*

Height of Land

Boasting one of the finest scenic turnouts on any road in Maine, Height of Land on Route 17, south of Oquossoc and north of Rumford, is a popular stop for those traveling to the Rangeley Lakes region. It is located where the road reaches its crest, some 2,247 feet above sea level on Spruce Mountain.

The pull-off is located on a 512-acre preserve protected by the Rangeley Lakes Heritage Trust. Recently improved by the state, it offers expansive views over hundreds of square miles to the Northwest out over Mooselookmeguntic Lake. The storied Appalachian Trail also crosses the road here. *Maine Atlas: M18, A4*

Doc Grant Restaurant Sign

Doc Grant's eatery opened in downtown Rangeley in 1941. It was shuttered while Elmer "Doc" Grant was away during World War II, but reopened in 1946 and was a fixture until it closed about twenty years ago. In 1957, Doc got the idea to put up a sign declaring his establishment straddled the halfway point between the Equator and North Pole. The sign continues to entertain visitors even though the actual 45th parallel is a couple of miles north of town. *Maine Atlas: M28, E5*

Rangeley Boat

During the Golden Age of fly fishing in the Rangeley Lakes Region, guides developed the distinctive cross between a canoe and a rowboat that can weather sudden storms and four-foot waves. Over time, unique features, such as closed oarlocks, round pivoting seats, and a square stern were added to the wood lapstrake "Rangeley Boat." A monument dedicated to the boats can be found at the Outdoor Sporting Heritage Museum in Oquossoc. *Maine Atlas: M28, E3*

Piazza Rock

Rangeley is an official "Appalachian Trail Town" and the famous, 2,200-mile footpath crosses Route 4 just south of town. As the trail ascends Saddleback Mountain it passes a distinctive overhanging, flat boulder known as Piazza Rock. At the campsite there, a two-hole outhouse named "Your Move" sports a cribbage board installed between the seats. *Maine Atlas: M19, A1*

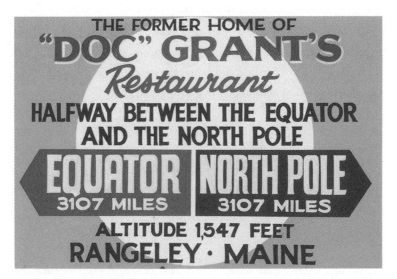

"Doc" Grant's Restaurant sign in Rangeley says the place is on the 45th parallel, but that latitude is actually several miles north of town.
Courtesy of Herb St. Johnsbury.

Covered Bridges

Covered bridges are a quintessential symbol of New England. In typical Yankee style, the spans were covered to afford the structure protection from the elements, making it easier to keep the decking free of snow and ice, and helping keep horses calm while crossing high over rushing streams.

At their high point, there were hundreds of covered bridges throughout the region, but most succumbed to old age, fire, or flood. Young lovers particularly liked the privacy afforded by these structures as a trip across a covered bridge was the perfect opportunity to steal a kiss.

Babb's Bridge, Presumpscot River, Built in 1843
Maine's oldest covered bridge. Babb's Bridge is located off River Road, two and a half miles north of South Windham, then one-half mile west between the towns of Gorham and Windham. It burned in 1973, but has since been rebuilt.

Hemlock Bridge, Saco River, Built in 1857
Hemlock Bridge is located off Route 302, three miles northwest of East Fryeburg in the town of Fryeburg. Spanning an old channel of the Saco River, it is of Paddleford truss construction with supporting laminated wooden arches.

Lowe's Bridge, Piscataquis River, Built in 1857
Lowe's Bridge, originally built in 1857, carried away by flood in 1987, and rebuilt in 1990, is located off Routes 6 and 15, three-quarters of a mile east and one mile north of Sangerville, between the towns of Sangerville and Guilford.

Lowe's Bridge over the Piscataquis River along Route 15 between Sangerville and Guilford was destroyed by a flood in 1987 and then rebuilt in 1990.
Photo Courtesy USGS.

Sunday River Bridge, Sunday River, Built in 1872

Sunday River Bridge, also known as the "Artist's Bridge," is the most painted and photographed bridge in the State of Maine. It is located off Routes 2 and 26, about four miles northwest of North Bethel in the town of Newry.

Porter Bridge, Ossipee River, Built in 1868

Porter Bridge, built by the towns of Porter and Parsonsfield as a joint project, is a two-span structure located off Route 160, one-half mile south of Porter. It was refurbished in 1999.

Robyville Bridge, Kenduskeag Stream, Built in 1876

The Robyville Bridge is the only completely shingled covered bridge in the State of Maine. It is located off Route 15 in Robyville Village in the town of Corinth, about three miles northwest of Kenduskeag Village.

A vintage postcard image of Artist's Covered Bridge over the Sunday River near Bethel. *From Author's Collection.*

Lovejoy Bridge, Ellis River, Built in 1883

Lovejoy Bridge, a Paddleford truss structure, at only seventy feet long, is the shortest of Maine's covered bridges. Built by the town of Andover, it is located off Route 5 at South Andover.

Bennet Bridge, Magalloway River, Built in 1901

Bennet Bridge is a relatively young bridge located off Route 16, one and a half miles south of the Wilsons Mills post office, then west three-tenths of a mile in Lincoln Plantation.

Watson Settlement Bridge, Meduxnekeag Stream, Built in 1911

Watson Settlement Bridge, located off Route 1 on the road to Woodstock from Littleton, in the town of Littleton, is the farthest north as well as the youngest covered bridge in the state.

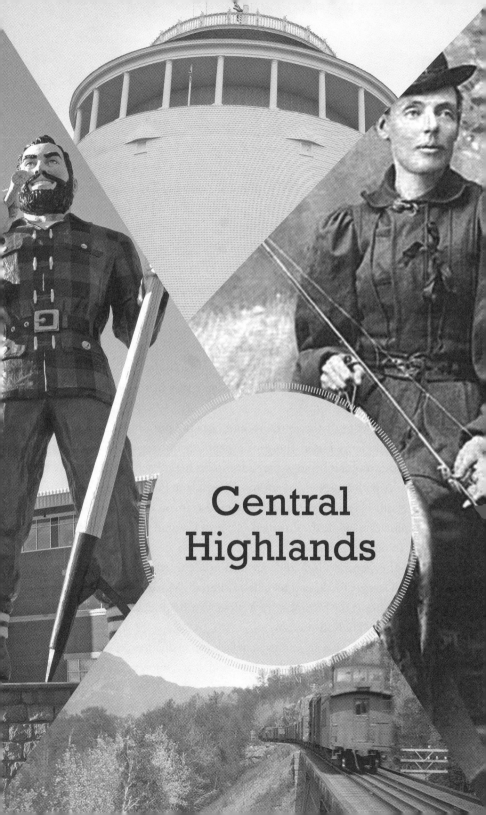

Central
Highlands

Central Highlands

From bustling cities such as Bangor and Waterville to vast working forests and preserves to the north, Maine's Central Highlands has long been home to people with industrious and ambitious natures.

Larger than life figures of bygone days abound including the legendary Stanley Brothers of Kingfield—who invented the "Stanley Steamer" automobile and developed dry plate photography.

Two knights, Sir Hiram Maxim, inventor of the machine gun, and Sir Harry Oakes, gold mine owner and entrepreneur, both hail from the village of Sangerville. Over in Farmington, Chester Greenwood, inventor of earmuffs, continues to be celebrated to this day. In Bangor, you can visit an actual piece of the ill-fated battleship *Maine*.

Maine's largest lake, Moosehead, commands the north. It is home to Mount Kineo, a towering flint edifice that has attracted visitors since prehistoric times.

Greenville, at the southern end, was the jumping-off place for many of Henry David Thoreau's expeditions and legions of explorers on snowmobiles begin winter adventures here. Each fall, East Cove bustles with scores of aircraft for the Seaplane Fly-in.

Gulf Hagas, often called the Grand Canyon of the East, invites exploration, while the drowned village of Flagstaff is visited most easily in our imaginations.

The Central Highlands are also home to Maine's largest boulder, Daggett Rock, and its tallest waterfall, Moxie Falls. The village of Phillips is the birthplace of Maine's first Registered Maine Guide, Cornelia "Fly Rod" Crosby.

Explore the woods southwest of Jackman to discover the site of a former German prisoner-of-war camp. And, if you know what it means to do "The Lucky Lindy!" remember that Canaan is home to the packing crate that brought the legendary *Spirit of St. Louis* back to America from France. It was recycled into a tiny, private Charles Lindbergh museum.

Opposite (clockwise from top): Thomas Hill Standpipe in Bangor *(From Author's Collection)*; Cornelia "Fly Rod" Crosby; Onawa Trestle on the CP Line *(From Bert Call Collection)*; and the Paul Bunyan statue in Bangor *(From Author's Collection)*.

A member of the notorious Brady Gang lies dead on Central Street in Bangor after a shootout with the FBI.
Courtesy of Digicommons.

Shootout on Central Street

One of Prohibition's downsides was a rise in crime. Even after repeal in 1933, the public remained gripped by news stories of celebrity gangsters such as John Dillinger, Baby Face Nelson, and Bonnie and Clyde. The FBI's efforts to catch these criminals prompted the creation of a top ten list of wanted criminals. In September 1937, Public Enemy Number One, Alfred James "Al" Brady and his gang, arrived in Bangor. By the time they arrived in the Queen City, they had killed four people and committed four murders, more than two hundred robberies and various other crimes.

Authorities were tipped off by an alert retail clerk at Dakin's Sporting Goods on Central Street after members of Brady's gang purchased, with cash, a pair of .45 caliber automatic handguns. A few days later, on October 5, gang member James Dalhover inquired at the store about purchasing a Thompson submachine gun. The clerk told him they were illegal, but that "some rum runners might have one," and he'd look into it.

The FBI was waiting for Dalhover when he returned and he was arrested by an agent posing as a clerk. When more than a dozen FBI agents and fifteen Maine and Indiana state troopers moved in to arrest the other gang members outside, Brady and Clarence Shaffer Jr. came out of their stolen car guns blazing. Both ended up dead in the street, their bodies riddled with more than sixty bullets. A granite block in the sidewalk commemorates the spot today.

Brady was buried without fanfare in Mount Hope Cemetery in Bangor. *Maine Atlas: M77, C3*

Always Remember the Maine!

The pride of the Navy's Great White Fleet, the battleship USS *Maine,* was shattered by a gigantic explosion while the batttleship was at anchor in Havana harbor on February 15, 1898. A total of 260 crew members were killed.

A US Naval Court of Inquiry ruled that the ship had been sunk by a mine. Newspapers of the day fanned the calls for war with giant headlines proclaiming "Remember the Maine! The Hell with Spain."

The incident, along with other points of tension, resulted in the outbreak of the Spanish-American War in April 1898.

An armistice three months later halted fighting, but not before Spain

USS *Maine.* The United States entered the Spanish-American War after the battleship USS *Maine* blew up in Havana Harbor in 1898.
Courtesy of Digicommons.

ceded Puerto Rico, Guam, and the Philippines to the United States.

Investigators using modern forensic techniques re-examined the cause in 1976 and determined the explosion was most likely caused by a fire in a coal bunker that ignited nearby ammunition.

In 1922, the USS *Maine* monument was created in Davenport Park on Main Street in Bangor. The granite edifice features the metal shield and scrollwork salvaged from the bow of the doomed battleship in 1912. *Maine Atlas: M77, C2*

Hidden Tank Quenches Town's Thirst

The Thomas Hill Standpipe in Bangor sits on the most prominent place in town. Although it appears to be a large wooden tower, that exterior structure encloses a massive water tank comprised of hundreds of wrought iron plates joined together with rivets. It can hold an astounding 1.5 million gallons of water.

Built in 1897, the tank itself stands fifty-feet high and is seventy-five feet across. The overall structure is 110 feet tall. Originally it was painted gray, but was changed to white when lights were added in 1912. During World War II, it was painted olive drab.

The popular destination was visited by thousands of visitors each year until it was closed in the 1940s, not long after a young boy died from a fall while climbing on interior beams. Today, four times annually, Bangor's water department opens the large deck atop the structure to visitors so they can enjoy the view of more than fifty miles. It is especially popular in the fall. *Maine Atlas: M77, C2*

Infamous Victorian Death Couch

Long before the name Hannibal was associated with "some fava beans and a nice chianti," folks in Maine automatically thought of Hannibal Hamlin, Abraham Lincoln's first vice president, a US senator and, ambassador to Spain. He was born in 1809 in Paris, Maine,

The couch upon which Hannibal Hamlin died. The couch is on display at the Bangor Public Library.
From Author's Collection.

while the state was still part of Massachusetts. His death, however, in 1891, remains immortalized by the couch upon which he "drew his last breath," now on display at the Bangor Public Library.

A farmer and newspaper editor, Hamlin eventually became a lawyer and moved to Hampden. He served in the Maine House of Representatives and aided with negotiations that helped end the Aroostook War in 1839.

While playing cards at Bangor's Tarratine Club on July 4, 1891, he collapsed and fell unconscious. Members put him on the couch to make him comfortable and, despite "a dose of brandy and ammonia that briefly revived him," he died a few hours later, his wife and a son by his side. A sign on the couch asks visitors to refrain from sitting on it. Considering what happened to the last person to do so, that is probably not a problem. *Maine Atlas: M77, C2*

Oh, The Horror!—Writer, That Is

A master of the macabre, Maine's own Stephen King made a house he and wife Tabitha purchased in 1979 on West Broadway in Bangor into a "shining" center of his creative empire that has included more than sixty-one novels that have sold more than 350 million copies. Many of his books and short stories have been made into movies.

King also owns nearby radio station WZON.

The Victorian mansion, built in 1858, is guarded by a wrought-iron fence that features spider web gates and finials that look like bats.

In 2019, Bangor city officials approved a zoning change to allow the home to be converted into a nonprofit writers' center, retreat and archive. *Maine Atlas: M77, C2*

The home of horror writer Stephen King in Bangor. *From Author's Collection.*

The Biggest and Best Bunyan—Ever

Standing proudly on the lawn at the Cross Insurance Center, Bangor's Paul Bunyan statue looks toward the mighty Penobscot River, the river which fueled the state's lumber boom and earned the town the moniker of "Queen City." The fiberglass over steel statue is considered the first, largest, and many say, the least creepy of several Bunyan statues that have sprung up around the country. It was designed by local artist J. Norman Martin.

Donated in 1959, about four

The Paul Bunyan statue located in front of the Cross Insurance Center in Bangor. *From Author's Collection.*

months before a similar-sized model in Oregon, the statue has been refurbished several times. To help cement Maine's claim to being the home of the legendary lumberman, officials in 1959 obtained a back-dated birth certificate claiming Bunyan was born in Bangor on February 12, 1859. *Maine Atlas: M77, D2*

Grand Canyon of the East

Tucked away in the deep woods above Milo is Gulf Hagas, the geological wonder known as the Grand Canyon of the East.

Carved by the West Branch of the Pleasant River, this National Natural Scenic Landmark extends for three miles, beginning in the north and flowing south through progressively higher walls of slate. At one point the cliffs, which are barely ten feet apart at the bottom, tower more than 130 feet above the river.

The passageway was even narrower a century before when logs were being driven downstream to fuel the furnaces at Katahdin Iron

Chester Greenwood of Farmington, who is credited with inventing the modern earmuffs.

Wonderful!
Cold Comfort Sparks Invention

Cold ears while ice skating was reportedly the inspiration for 15-year-old Chester Greenwood of Farmington to ask his grandmother to sew tuffs of beaver fur to a wire hoop to create the world's first set of earmuffs in 1873. He got a patent on the idea at age 19. His company continued to make them for more than sixty years. In 1936 alone, they made and shipped 400,000 pairs.

The mechanically inclined Greenwood also started a bicycle business, helped create the town's first telephone network, and tinkered with heating system technology. He held a patent for a wide-bottom tea kettle, a steel rake, and a machine used to manufacture steel wire and thread.

Maine celebrated its first Chester Greenwood Day on December 21, 1977. A parade in Greenwood's honor is still held on the first Saturday of December in Farmington.

Maine Atlas: M79, B1

Works. Loggers eventually used explosives to widen the choke points to reduce the number of dangerous log jams.

A long, rugged loop trail follows the canyon's east side. This rim trail passes through the Hermitage, one of the last remaining stands of old-growth forest in New England. There are limited places to access the river. The Appalachian Trail also passes close to the Gulf. *Maine Atlas: M42, D1*

Katahdin Iron Works

Little but the foundation of an early smelting furnace remains of the bustling manufacturing operation and town that once thrived at Katahdin Iron Works.

For forty years, beginning in 1843, red iron oxide quarried from nearby Ore Mountain was hauled to furnaces at the Works where it was heated to remove sulfur. The ore, limestone, and charcoal were dumped into the top of the blast furnace to create pig iron. In the 1880s, as much as twenty tons of the metal were produced at the works each day.

The charcoal kilns at the facility used a lot of wood. More than 20,000 cords, all harvested in the surrounding forests, were burned annually.

For a while, hotels at nearby Silver Lake, catered to tourists and visitors that arrived en masse by railroad. The site of the furnace and one remaining kiln are now operated by the State of Maine as historic site. It is a popular snowmobiling destination. *Maine Atlas: M42, D2*

Record-Setting Rock

Considered the largest glacial erratic boulder in the State of Maine, Daggett Rock in Phillips is believed to weigh eight thousand tons— more than three thousand times heavier than the average block of stone used to build the Great Pyramid at Giza.

An early postcard view of Maine's largest boulder, Daggett Rock, before trees reclaimed the area. *From Author's Collection.*

The massive glacial ice sheet that covered all of Maine is thought to have plucked it from the Saddleback Mountain area, many miles to the north. In its current position it is split into three sections.

Legend holds that the rock split two centuries ago when a woodsman named Daggett, who had been drinking, climbed atop it during a thunderstorm. Moments after he reportedly took the Almighty's name in vain, he and the rock were hit by a massive bolt of lightning sending him off to his not-so-heavenly reward and leaving the boulder in three pieces.

Daggett Rock is located up a short hiking trail off the unpaved Wheeler Hill Road in Phillips. *Maine Atlas: M19, A4*

Maine's Hometown Knights

Plenty of colonial-era individuals with ties to Maine have been knighted by various governments and monarchs over the years. They include Chief Nescambious of the Maliseet tribe of the Abenaki, knighted by French King Louis XIV in 1706, and the state's first knight, William Phips of Sheepscot, knighted by King James II, in

1687 for recovering Spanish treasure.

Perhaps Maine's two most famous knights remarkably hail from the same hometown—Sangerville. They are Sir Hiram Maxim, inventor of the machine gun and Sir Harry Oakes.

Maxim, who was nominated by Queen Victoria, was knighted by King Edward VII in 1901. Oakes was born in Sangerville in 1874. Leaving Maine at a young age, he spent sixteen years traveling the world in the search of gold. During that sojourn he was shipwrecked on the Alaskan coast and held prisoner by Russians. He finally struck it rich in Ontario, earning as much as $60,000 a day in 1911. King George VI knighted him in 1939 for donations to charity.

Oakes, who also had a mansion in Bar Harbor that is today part of the Atlantic Oceanside Hotel, was bludgeoned to death at his estate in the Bahamas in 1943. No one was ever charged in the killing. *Maine Atlas: M31, C5*

Two Towns That Drowned

The completion of Long Falls Dam, the largest in Maine, on the Dead River resulted in the creation of Flagstaff Lake, Maine's fourth largest. As the water rose in 1950, however, it inundated two communities, including Flagstaff Village and Dead River. Most residents sold out to Central Maine Power Company and some homes and a chapel were moved to Eustis. More than three hundred bodies buried in two local cemeteries were exhumed and relocated.

Flagstaff was named for the flagpole reportedly erected by Benedict Arnold during his ill-fated expedition to attack Quebec in 1775. Settlers, including a descendant of Pilgrim Miles Standish, arrived in the early 1800s.

Water up to fifty feet deep now covers the long-lost towns. Also at the bottom of the lake lie two US Air Force jets that crashed after colliding on a training mission in November 1959. *Maine Atlas: M29, B3*

The Incomparable 'Fly Rod' Crosby

Seeking to improve the reputation of wilderness guides in the state, the Maine Legislature passed a bill in 1897 requiring licensing. License number one was issued to Cornelia "Fly Rod" Crosby of Phillips, a woman famous for promoting the wonders of Maine's outdoors at shows and exhibitions along the Eastern Seaboard. Back when environmental and conservation sentiments were not as strong as today, Crosby reportedly caught more than 200 fish (catch and release of course!) in a single day near Rangeley. She also shot the last caribou legally taken in Maine.

A friend of the legendary Annie Oakley, as well as guide to President Teddy Roosevelt, Crosby wrote for sporting publications under the name "Fly Rod" for decades.

She died at the ripe old age of 91 in Strong, Maine, in 1946. *Maine Atlas: M19, B3*

Maine's Famous Flying Fisherman

"Gadabout" Gaddis, television's incomparable "Flying Fisherman," settled in Bingham and established his own airport there.
From Author's Collection.

Long before Bassmaster Bill Nance or other televangelists of the rod and reel lifestyle, there was Roscoe Vernon "Gadabout" Gaddis, The Flying Fisherman who eventually settled in Bingham.

Tooling around North America in his beloved Piper Cherokee plane, the cowboy-hat wearing Gaddis combined his love of fishing and flying and shared them via a series of shows including *Outdoors with Liberty Mutual, Going*

Places with Gadabout Gaddis, and ultimately, *The Flying Fisherman*. Far from today's slickly produced fare, Gaddis did it with a single cameraman, who filmed from a second boat or canoe. They didn't record sound, instead adding narration later. If he didn't catch a single fish in five days of filming, well, they showed that, too.

Eventually Gaddis expanded his outdoors empire to include fishing gear, a book, and posters. He eventually purchased the local airport which was renamed Gadabout Gaddis Field and is now home to North Maine Rivers Rafting. The Maine Aeronautics Association named their major service award the Gadabout Gaddis Cup. Gaddis went to that great trout stream in the sky in 1986 at age 90. *Maine Atlas: M30, D4*

Avoiding the Highways to Hell

They say the road to hell is paved with good intentions, but at several spots in Maine large signs admonish motorists to avoid having Maine emulate that high-temperature destination at all costs.

The original sign stated "Keep Maine Green. THIS IS GOD'S COUNTRY. WHY SET IT ON FIRE AND MAKE IT LOOK LIKE HELL." It was erected on the road to Kokadjo (population, not many), just north of Greenville, by the Maine Forest Service and Civilian Conservation Corps workers in the 1930s.

Farther to the west, in Highland Plantation (again, population, not many) near Bingham, opponents of a proposal to erect thirty-nine power-generating windmills on a scenic ridge continued with that theme, erecting a sign along the main dirt access road in 2011. The original proposal was withdrawn but another surfaced in 2015. *Maine Atlas: M41, B4*

Maine's Not-So-Great Escape

Maine hosted several prisoner-of-war camps during World War II, including facilities in Aroostook and Washington counties and one near Jackman. The Hobbstown Camp near Spencer Lake, which housed more than three hundred Germans, was the scene of a failed escape attempt when three young prisoners took off from an ice-harvesting work detail on March 7, 1945. Planning their escape well in advance, they squirreled away meager rations and fashioned crude snowshoes. A compass made from a magnetized needle and peach can worked "as well as one from L.L.Bean," according to a 2014 article in *Down East* Magazine.

The escape launched one of the largest manhunts in Maine history with nearly three aircraft and fifty law enforcement personnel, including state police, game wardens, and the FBI.

In the end, it was the lingering Maine winter that proved to be the escapee's toughest adversary. As predicted by a local hermit familiar with the area, the terrain and icy conditions forced the prisoners toward the Forks area where they were caught shivering in a makeshift lean-to five days later.

Children from the Forest Hills School in Jackman raised funds to erect a monument at the overgrown site of the Hobbstown Camp in 2006. *Maine Atlas: M39, D4*

Scenic Byway Offers Road Trip to Past

Stretching seventy-eight miles along the Kennebec River from Solon to the Canadian border north of Jackman, the Old Canada Road Scenic Byway along US 201 follows a general route that settlers, loggers, and Benedict Arnold's ill-fated expedition to attack Quebec City in 1775 took in years gone past.

Numerous sites along the way show signs of habitation by Native Americans followed by early French and English settlers and missionaries. While today's modern highway has obliterated much of the earlier road, the woods and hills are home to numerous abandoned cellar holes and old wood mill sites.

The first official road was authorized in 1817 and the area's wealth of timber and rich farmland attracted more and more people to the area. Markers describing historic events line the route today.

The area's historic resources and spectacular scenery resulted in the route being declared a National Scenic Byway in 2000. *Maine Atlas: M40, C1*

Thoreau's Guides to the Maine Woods

Writer Henry David Thoreau won acclaim for a series of essays later published as *The Maine Woods*. His multiple excursions up through Moosehead, down the West and East branches of Penobscot, up Katahdin, and to the Allagash, would never have been possible without the wisdom and labor of his guides, in particular, Native Americans Joseph Attean and Joe Polis.

Attean was born on Christmas Day in 1829 and died in a river driving accident on the Penobscot on July 4, 1870. He was the last full hereditary Chief of the Penobscots as well as the tribe's first elected chief. He famously took Thoreau moose hunting.

A plaque overlooking Attean Pond near Jackman recounts his exploits, although he never traveled there and the pond is not named for him.

Joe Polis also served as a chief of the Penobscot Nation. He taught Thoreau how to run rapids in a canoe and much about native plants and their uses.

Thoreau's last words were "moose" and "Indian." Ralph Waldo Emerson who gave the eulogy at the funeral said Thoreau admired three men, Walt Whitman, abolitionist John Brown, and Joe Polis. *Maine Atlas: M33, E4*

Big as an Ox—Times Two

The expression "as big as an ox" dates back far into our agrarian past, but it took on special meaning in the early years of the 1900s when a pair of oxen from Maine were declared the largest in the world.

Named "Katahdin," and "Granger" by farmer Alphonso Rand of Stetson, this pair of draft animals were the tractors of their day, helping pull stumps, move rocks, and haul logs.

The team quickly began winning ribbons at agricultural fairs and by the age of two weighed a combined 6,600 pounds. They continued to grow until Granger alone weighed 4,800 pounds and Katahdin topped out at 5,000 pounds. Taken to Madison Square Garden in New York in 1906 they caused quite a commotion walking around downtown Manhattan.

After Katahdin died at age eleven, Rand had him stuffed and mounted and continued to display him at parades and events. The truck-mounted exhibit was destroyed in a barn fire in 1934. Granger lived to be seventeen. *Maine Atlas: M22, A3*

The world's largest pair of oxen, Katahdin and Granger, in Stetson.
Courtesy of Stetson Historical Society.

Longest Canoe and Guinness, Too

Guided by teacher Harold Whitten, students and other teachers at Nokomis High in Newport constructed the world's longest canoe as a school project in 2006. It was built in eighteen prefabricated eight-foot sections and when fastened together at the landing on Sebasticook Lake it measured 149 feet and one inch long. It reportedly beat the previous world record holder by thirty-two feet.

Crewed by thirty-six intrepid paddlers, the maiden voyage on Saturday, June 10 didn't last long—about four minutes. The vessel got about one hundred feet from the dock before, much like the Titanic, it broke into two pieces. The canoe project was designed to be a fundraiser to pay for a pontoon boat to take disabled people for trips on area lakes. *Maine Atlas: M22, A1*

Going Back to Not-So-Square One

There's no underestimating the hardships endured by early land surveyors in the State of Maine. Using rudimentary equipment such as a transit and steel chains, crews were expected to keep their lines perfectly straight over enormous distances. Towns were laid out organically in the southern part of the state, but the vast tracts to the north were eyed for a formal grid.

In 1825, surveyor Joseph Norris Sr., was tasked with laying out an east to west transect called the Monument Line from the St. Croix River in the east, then due west ninety miles. That quest took him through the wildest country in the state, including up and over part of the Katahdin mastiff.

The monument line and the state's eastern border became a jumping-off place for the creating of grids of townships and ranges. Townships are designated by letters and numbers. T2, R9 means the second row of townships and the ninth column. There are also a series of twenty suffixes that further identify the region.

After centuries of conflicting claims, multiple owners, frequent sales, inaccurate surveys, and shifting boundaries, it is no surprise the grid is far from perfect. The result was numerous triangular pieces of land referred to in the industry as "gores," after the tips of medieval spears.

Maine has several that have taken on mythical status as unique places to visit. They include Blake Gore near Moose River, Coburn Gore near Eustis, Gorham Gore near Jackman, Hibberts Gore near Washington, Massachusetts Gore north of Jackman, Misery Gore near Rockwood, Moxie Gore near The Forks, and Veazie Gore near Millinocket. *Maine Atlas: M41, A1*

Tallest Waterfall Flows with Gumption

The highest cascade in Maine, and one of the highest in New England, Moxie Falls, located in Moxie Gore, near The Forks, plunges more than ninety feet into a deep pool below. There's no connection to the fabled soft drink of the same name, although some might argue the dark, tannin-stained water looks like Moxie. In fact, Moxie is the Abenaki word for "dark water."

The falls, located on an easy to moderate hiking trail to a nice viewing platform, is on Moxie Stream—which drains Moxie Pond allowing its waters to flow into the Kennebec River. Whitewater rafters running the Kennebec Gorge, sometimes stop and make a half-mile trek to the base of the falls.

Although the stream above the falls may appear an inviting place to swim officials discourage it. A man died in 2005 while trying to rescue a female companion who got caught up in the current and pulled over the falls. She was severely injured but survived. *Maine Atlas: M40, E3*

Maine's Conscience of the Senate

Margaret Madeline Chase Smith, of Skowhegan, was the first woman to serve in both houses of the US Congress and the first female elected to either office from Maine.

In 1964, the lifelong Republican was also the first woman from either party to be nominated to run for president. Smith, a former teacher, telephone operator, and high school basketball coach, began her career in national politics helping in the Washington, D.C., office of her husband, US Rep. Clyde Smith. Upon his untimely death, she ran for the seat and won handily.

She is best known for her famous "Declaration of Conscience" speech in 1950 in which she stood up to oppose McCarthyism. While criticizing the Democratic administration she wrote "… I don't want to see the Republican Party ride to political victory on the Four Horsemen of Calumny—Fear, Ignorance, Bigotry, and Smear."

Smith's legacy is preserved by the Margaret Chase Smith Library in Skowhegan and in the Margaret Chase Smith Policy Center at the University of Maine. *Maine Atlas: M80, A1*

Tallest Trestle Spans Tiny Brook

Onawa Trestle, located on the Canadian Pacific Railroad line just east of Borestone Mountain in Elliotsville Township, is the tallest and longest such structure in Maine. It carries a single track some 130 feet above the relatively small Ship Pond Stream. The bridge spans a distance of 1,230 feet—nearly a quarter of a mile.

Several iterations of the bridge have stood on the site. The first was made entirely of wood in 1887. The second, built in 1896, was of more stalwart iron construction. The current bridge, which features tall concrete pillars supporting steel trusses and girders, was completed in 1931.

The Canadian Pacific Line, which runs more than 230 miles from the former village of Holeb in the west, to Vanceboro in the east, provides a speedy connection between the provinces of Quebec and New Brunswick. A head-on crash between freight and passenger trains near the trestle in 1919 resulted in 23 fatalities. *Maine Atlas: M41, E5*

Pollywog Gorge's Gruesome Toll

While not as spectacular as Gulf Hagas located to the south, Pollywog Gorge, on the Appalachian Trail in the Nahmakanta Public Reserve Lands, is an impressive geological wonder. The mile-long chasm, with the tumbling waters of Pollywog Stream at the bottom, features walls some 180 feet high. The best way to view down into the gorge is from the Appalachian Trail, which follows the east side for much of the gorge's length. There is a small, unfenced viewing area which is not recommended for those with a fear of heights. When trees are leafed out, there's little to see.

During the early 1900s, loggers constructed dams throughout the watershed, including several small dams in the gorge to assist in moving logs cut on the surrounding cliffs which were unceremoniously rolled into the chasm during the spring freshet. More than a dozen river drivers lost their lives to accidents in the gorge over the years. Several are reportedly buried in unmarked graves along its banks. *Maine Atlas: M50, E2*

Diamond in Rough Breaks Baseball Barrier

Old Town's Louis Sockalexis, a Penobscot, was the first Native American and the first member of a minority to play baseball in the National League. He joined the Cleveland Spiders in 1897, some five decades before Jackie Robinson shattered the sport's color barrier.

Growing up on Indian Island, Sockalexis' athletic abilities were apparent early. He played semi-pro ball with teams in Maine during his teen years into his early 20s. He later played for St. Mary's College of Van Buren, Ricker Classical Institute in Houlton, a team at the Poland Spring resort, and eventually Holy Cross in Worcester, Massachusetts, and Notre Dame before being tapped by the Spiders in 1897. Partially based on Sockalexis' star power fueled by his impressive hitting, fielding, and base-running, newspapers of the day began referring to the team as the Indians.

After wrestling with alcohol addiction and health issues, Sockalexis ended his professional sports career, returning to Old Town in the early 1900s. He died at the age of 42 while working as a logger.

A postcard image of professional baseball player Louis Sockalexis, a member of the Penobscot Tribe. *From Author's Collection.*

The 2,500-seat Sockalexis Ice Arena on Indian Island is named in his honor. He was inducted into the Maine Sports Hall of Fame in 1985, joining his cousin, Andrew Sockalexis who won a gold medal for the marathon in the 1912 Olympics. *Maine Atlas: M33, E4*

Crate Cradles Spirit of Aviation First

Folks in Maine are steadfastly reticent to toss aside anything that might prove useful in the future. That spirit of waste-not, want-not extends back to Charles Lindbergh's incredible first-ever solo flight across the Atlantic Ocean. The packing crate used to return the *Spirit of St. Louis* to America in 1927 can be found in Canaan, Maine, where it has become a defacto museum of sorts, although shifting circumstances have resulted in it not currently being open to the public.

The 290-square-foot wood box was first shipped to New Hampshire and turned into a camp. It was moved to Maine in 1990. It has been added onto over the years and now looks more like a small cottage. Inside, owner Larry Ross has collected numerous Lindbergh photographs and memorabilia along with testimonials and statements from people who knew or met the intrepid aviator. A granite monument honoring Lindbergh is located on the grounds. *Maine Atlas: M21, B3*

Tiny Tower Looms Large in Forestry

A tiny log cabin with a platform on the roof, on the southernmost peak of Squaw Mountain (since renamed to Moose Mountain) near Greenville was the first fire tower in Maine and the very first manned tower in the country.

The first structure on the spot was erected in June 1905 by a local lumber company hoping to get early warning of any major conflagrations.

They had reason to worry. A newspaper account in August of that year reported, "In the Moosehead region the watchman on Squaw Mountain lookout station reports a big fire about fifty miles distant on the waters of the north branch of the Penobscot. There is another quite sizable blaze on Russell . . . Still another fire is . . . is burning furiously."

The first steel tower was installed in 1919. The last steel-legged tower was put up in 1959. One major restoration was done in 1985. In 2011, a Maine Forest Service helicopter crew removed the tower frame to the grounds of the Natural Resource Education Center on Route 15 in Greenville where the cab was re-created to 1958 plans. The fully restored tower is now open to the public at the Center. *Maine Atlas: M41, D2*

Memorial Recalls Wintry Crash

At the height of the Cold War, in January 1963, a Strategic Air Command B52 bomber on a low-level training run literally fell out of the sky at Elephant Mountain, just east of Greenville.

Unbeknownst to the crew the tall vertical stabilizer on the tail had broken off in turbulence resulting in the crew having only a few seconds to abandon the doomed aircraft. Only the pilot, co-pilot, and navigator, who had ejection seats, were able to get out. Six other crewmen did not.

The copilot died when he struck a tree. The pilot and navigator were seriously injured, but found themselves alone in the dark with temperatures hovering around minus 30 gedrees Fahrenheit. Searchers, who used snowplows to remove fifteen-foot-deep drifts on the roads leading to the area, were able to reach and evacuate the survivors the next day. Investigators eventually found the tail section one and a half miles away on the eastern side of the mountain.

The debris-strewn hillside remains a memorial to this day. A local snowmobile and hiking trail leads to a slate monument, a section of the plane's tail, and pieces of landing gear.

The Moosehead Riders Snowmobile Club has repeatedly honored the crew's memory. Two ejection seats and other items are on display at the Moosehead Historical Society on Pritham Avenue in Greenville. *Maine Atlas: M41, C4*

Beloved 'Kate' is Keeper of Lake's History

For more than one hundred years the steamboat *Katahdin* has plied the waters of Maine's largest lake—Moosehead.

Built in 1914 at Bath Iron Works, the vessel was hauled in sections by rail and oxen to Greenville to begin serving the lake's bustling tourist trade. Multiple trips hauling up to five hundred passengers and freight were made each day between Greenville and resorts at Kineo

The restored steamboat Katahdin makes regular excursion runs on Maine's largest lake, Moosehead, during the summer season.
From Author's Collection.

and other locations around the forty-mile lake.

At more than 102 feet long, the steel-hulled *Kate* as she is affectionately known, draws just over three feet of water. Originally powered by a steam boiler, she is the oldest vessel built in Bath still afloat.

As the resort era faded in 1940, the *Katahdin* was converted to diesel power and used to tow rafts of pulpwood across the lake. She was mothballed as an exhibit in 1976, but eventually restored. Now offering regular cruises on the lake from the Moosehead Marine Museum, the *Katahdin* received new engines in the fall of 2019. *Maine Atlas: M41, D2*

Maine's Father of the Machine Gun

One of the late nineteenth century's most prolific inventors, Sir Hiram Maxim, a native of Sangerville, applied his genius to everything from automatic fire sprinkler systems, to amusement rides, to flying machines to the incandescent lightbulb—an idea, he claims,

A postcard image of Hiram Maxim from Sangerville posing with his greatest invention, the machine gun. *From Author's Collection.*

that was stolen by Thomas Edison.

But primarily, Maxim is remembered as inventor of the 500-shot-per-minute machine gun which he created in 1884. It was the first gun to use energy from the previous round to prepare the mechanism for the next shot. He and Edward Vickers went on to produce machine guns in England.

While testing his designs in his garden, he reportedly ran announcements in local newspapers warning neighbors to keep their windows open to avoid broken glass.

Later in life he suffered from deafness believed to be related to years of exposure to automatic gunfire.

Despite a messy personal life, Maxim was bestowed a knighthood by Queen Victoria in 1900, but was invested by King Edward VII after Victoria died shortly before the ceremony.

In recent years, the Hiram Maxim Historical Society has sponsored an annual shootout and expo in Dover-Foxcroft. *Maine Atlas: M31, C5*

Waterville's Two Cent Bridge was built in 1901 to provide pedestrian access for workers to reach a paper mill in Winslow. The toll remained just two cents from 1903 until 1960. *Courtesy of National Park Service.*

Two Cent Toll Eased Commute

Who doesn't like giving their two cents' worth? Well, that's exactly what it cost for pedestrians to cross this iron truss bridge over the Kennebec River in Waterville back in 1903.

Originally opened in late 1901, the first steel cable footbridge at the spot, designed by Edwin Dwight Graves for the Ticonic Foot Bridge Company, cost only a penny to cross. It provided vital access to residents of Waterville who needed to get to the paper mills in Winslow, but it was washed away by spring floods. The toll was raised to two cents when a new, sturdier bridge, some four hundred feet long and six feet wide, was built in 1903; the amount eventually lending its name to the structure. The toll remained at that level until abolished when the bridge was given to the City of Waterville in 1960. The bridge, located at the end of Temple Street, was added to the National Register of Historic Places in 1973.

In 1990, hundreds of concertgoers crowded onto the bridge causing serious damage that required closure. Repairs took several years. It was restored in its entirety in 2012. *Maine Atlas: M76, C2*

Wire Span Has Murky Origins

Controversy swirls over exactly who gets credit for building the Wire Bridge in New Portland over the Carrabassett River. The only survivor of four such bridges built in Maine in the mid-1800s, records about its construction are few and far between. One account says it was built in 1842 by a local engineer, Colonel F.B. Morse, who ordered the cables from England and had them hauled overland from Hallowell by teams of oxen. Some residents reportedly called the project "Morse's Fool Bridge."

But, according to a town history, work on the span designed and built by David Elder and Captain Charles Clark actually began in 1864 and took two years to finish. "It is impossible to be certain of the bridge's early history," states the application that put the bridge on the National Register of Historic Places.

The main span, which can carry three tons, is 188 feet long and 12 feet wide. Wood-frame towers that hold the steel cables rest on granite blocks. The towers are covered by shingles for weather protection. Concrete and granite blocks weighing thirty tons anchor the cables. About one hundred vehicles on the Wire Bridge Road use the span daily. *Maine Atlas: M20, A1*

Giant Pan Brings Home the Bacon

World-record frying pans seem to be everywhere these days, but Maine was not about to be left out of this sizzling category. While it has yet to be recognized by the ultimate arbiter of trivial pursuits—the *Guinness Book of World Records*—the town of Pittsfield claims to be the home of the World's Largest Non-Stick Frying Pan.

Some ten feet across, and made of aluminum instead of cast iron, it

Reported to be the largest non-stick frying pan in the world, this ten-foot beauty is used during Pittsfield's Annual Central Maine Egg Festival.
Courtesy of Central Maine Egg Festival.

is brought out of retirement each year and hauled to Manson Park for the Central Maine Egg Festival. It weighs some three hundred pounds.

The festival, which attracts as many as 35,000 people annually, bills itself as a celebration of the brown egg industry and features breakfast, chicken barbeque, street dance, parade, craft fair, "Egglympics," and fireworks.

According to the Pittsfield Historical Society it was made by Alcoa and coated with Teflon at DuPont's New Jersey plant. It made its first appearance at the festival on Aug. 10, 1983. Special gas burners were also constructed to make it fully functional. *Maine Atlas: M21, B5*

Kineo Looms Large on Biggest Lake

Looming straight up out of the depths of Moosehead Lake, Maine's largest freshwater body, Mount Kineo is located on a peninsula that nearly cuts the lake in half. In fact, cliffs on the southeast face loom some seven hundred feet above the surface although at their base is the deepest part of the lake, the bottom being some 246 feet below.

Native Americans were drawn to Kineo for its rhyolite rock (the largest deposit of its type in the United States) which has the same properties as flint. It made perfect arrowheads and other implements and was traded with tribes from New York to New Brunswick. Henry David Thoreau camped at Kineo.

The southern slopes of the peninsula have sported hotels and cottages since the mid-1800s. With rooms for five hundred guests, the Kineo House in 1911 was the largest inland waterfront hotel in America. The Mount Kineo Golf Course is believed to be the second oldest in the country. The resort faded quickly once rail service to Rockwood, west across the narrows, ended in the early 1930s.

In winter, as many as three thousand snowmobiles a day cross the frozen lake between Kineo and Rockwood.

Much of the area is now part of Mount Kineo State Park. In season there is regular water shuttle service from Rockwood.
Maine Atlas: M41, A1

Statue to Native People Stands Tall

Dedicated to Maine's Native Americans, Bernard Langlais' Indian Statue in Skowhegan is considered the tallest in the world. It was created and erected in 1969 to commemorate Maine's Sesquicentennial. Sitting atop a twenty-foot base, Langlais' creation, made of individual pieces of wood over a metal frame, depicts an individual with spear and grid representing a fish weir, similar to what would have been used in the nearby Kennebec River. The statue alone is sixty-nine-feet high, not counting the base. A sign on the back reads "Dedicated to the Maine Indians, the first people to use these lands in peaceful ways." It can be found in a tiny park, tucked away at the

SKOWHEGAN INDIAN
THIS SCULPTURE IS DEDICATED
TO THE MAINE INDIANS
THE FIRST PEOPLE TO USE
THESE LANDS IN PEACEFUL WAYS

The famous Indian Statue created by Bernard Langlais has been a landmark in Skowhegan for more than fifty years.
Courtesy of Kevin Bennett.

rear of a parking lot off High Street.

Langlais, a native of Old Town, left a long legacy of sculptures, paintings and other works around the state. He had been a student at the Skowhegan School of Painting and Sculpture and took three years to craft the statue while living in Cushing on the coast.

Coordinated by Colby College and the Kohler Foundation, the Langlais Trail celebrates his art with a self-guided tour and map of places where his work can be seen around Maine. The school also promotes the Langlais Sculpture Preserve at 576 River Road in Cushing. It is owned and operated by the George's River Land Trust. With more than sixty examples of his work, it features a satirical sculpture of Richard Nixon flashing a peace sign and a piece called "Local Girl" depicting Christina Olson, the local woman featured in Andrew Wyeth's seminal painting "Christina's World."

Langlais died in 1977 at the age of 56. *Maine Atlas: M21, B1*

The Stanleys

The Stanleys of Kingfield: Yankee Ingenuity at Work

Twin brothers Francis Edgar (F.E.) and Freelan Oscar (F.O.) Stanley were born in Kingfield, Maine, in 1849. Graduates of what is now the University of Maine at Farmington, they went into teaching, but soon turned to follow their inventive and industrious natures. They built and produced record-holding early steam cars, invented the artists' airbrush, and created dry plate photography, which revolutionized that industry. The former Kingfield Elementary School on School Street in Kingfield houses the story of the Stanley family including numerous artifacts, inventions, images and a collection of steam cars. *Maine Atlas: M30, E1*

Stanley Steamer

At their factory in Newton, Massachusetts, the Stanley brothers began manufacturing their steam car in 1897. They continued to make numerous models for nearly thirty years. Their steam car was the first motorized vehicle to climb Mount Washington, taking nearly two hours to cover the seven and a half miles to the summit of New England's highest mountain.

Stanley Rocket

In 1906, a Stanley Steamer set the World Speed Record when the "Stanley Rocket" covered a mile on a Florida beach in just 28.2 seconds for a speed of 127.65 miles per hour. It held that record for four years.

Airbrush

F.E. Stanley invented the commercial airbrush which used compressed air to atomize paint to assist him in his early portrait business. Among his more famous commissions were Henry Wadsworth Longfellow and William Cullen Bryant.

Opposite (clockwise from top): The Stanley Museum in Kingfield, Maine (From Author's Collection); Chansonetta Stanley Emmons (Courtesy of Digicommons); and Francis and Freelan Stanley riding in one of their famous steam-powered cars (Courtesy of the Stanley Museum).

Violins

Inspired by an uncle, F.O. Stanley crafted his first violin in Kingfield at the age of 11 in 1860. Both brothers and a nephew, Carlton Stanley, built many of the instruments. Later, in 1924, he started a company, run by Carlton, that produced more than five hundred violins.

Dry Plate Photography

Seeking to streamline the photo process, the Stanley brothers invented dry plate, photography which eliminated the need for creating a plate with chemicals immediately before exposure. In 1886, they patented a machine capable of coating a new plate every second. Eventually, they sold the company for the then princely sum of $500,000 to George Eastman, who founded camera and film giant Kodak.

Stanley Hotel

After building the Stanley Hotel in Estes Park, Colorado, F.O. Stanley designed and built the "Mountain Wagon," a thirty-horsepower steam bus capable of delivering guests and cargo to the facility. The hotel inspired Maine author Stephen King to write *The Shining* after he stayed there. A television miniseries of that name was filmed at the "Stanley," as were scenes for the film *Dumb and Dumber*.

Chansonetta Emmons

While the accomplishments of the Stanley Brothers are widely known, their sister Chansonetta was also an artistic genius. She was the only girl born into the family of six boys. A teacher with an interest in art, she eventually became an accomplished photographer who developed, printed, and framed her own work. She traveled throughout the Northeast and shared images of rural American life at lectures and exhibitions.

S T A N L E Y   S T E A M   C A R

THE FASTEST CAR IN THE WORLD
(Rate of 127.66 Miles an Hour)

NOTE—While Mr. Stanley appears in the driver's seat, this record breaking car was driven by Fred H. Marriott of Newton, Mass.

This car, at Ormond, Fla., Jan. 21 to 28, 1906, established the following World's Records:

WORLD'S RECORDS								FORMER RECORDS							
1 Kilometre	-	-	-	-	-	-	.18⅘	Darracq	-	-	-	-	-	-	.21⅘
1 Mile	-	-	-	-	-	-	.28⅘	Napier	-	-	-	-	-	-	.34⅘
1 Mile in Competition	-	-	-	-	-	.31⅘									.41⅘
5 Miles	-	-	-	-	-	-	2.47⅘	Napier	-	-	-	-	-	-	3.17⅘
2 Miles (World's record for cars eligible under the rules)					.59⅘										

The 5-mile record was made in competition, with a scoring start, and was at the rate of a mile in 33⅘ seconds, which is faster than any gasoline car built according to A. A. A. rules ever made for a single mile.

The power-plant in this car is exactly like that in the regular Stanley cars, except that it is larger, of about twice the power as the Touring Cars (Model F). It weighs 1,600 pounds, and has margin enough for another boiler of the same size (512 pounds) without passing the racing weight-limit of 2,204 pounds. The boiler is 30 inches in diameter and 18 inches deep. It contains 1,475 tubes, and has a total heating surface of 285 square feet. A steam pressure of 800 to 900 pounds is carried. The engine is 4½ x 6¼, and makes 350 revolutions to the mile. The wheels are 34 inches in diameter, and make 600 revolutions to the mile. They are equipped with 3-inch G. and J. tires. The body is so designed that the largest cross-section it presents, including the wheels, is only 9 square feet.

Above (top): An early Stanley Steamer makes its way up the treacherous auto road to the top of Mount Washington (Courtesy of Wikicommons); (bottom) An advertisement for the Stanley Brothers' world record steam-powered racing car.

Satan In the Woods & the Deep Blue Sea

Like much of Puritan New England, Maine has always held a fascination with the devil. There was no better way to ward off interlopers or display disdain than to black mark someplace with devil in the name or invoke the prospect of hell. From rock formations along Maine's southern coast, to chasms in the deepest woods, any place that was dark, geologically unique, or out of the ordinary became linked to the hand of Satan. Some tales involving encounters with Lucifer took on a true unique Maine flair. While fire and brimstone figure in many of the stories, so does the cold. One legend from the Milo area tells of the devil leaving snowshoe tracks in the rocks.

Hell's Half Acre, Bangor

Located between Front and Broad streets, near where they intersect with Union Street, Hell's Half Acre was, according to *Bangor Daily News* writer Wayne Reilly, "a place where loggers, sailors and other workingmen gathered to spend their cash on whiskey and women. Many of these men were transients, often immigrants, who traveled with jobs and the seasons."

Although Maine adopted prohibition early, liquor flowed freely in the saloons and brothels there where fights and other acts of violence occurred often.

Maine Atlas: M77, C2

Devil's Ovens, Bar Harbor

Located on a rocky shore that is inaccessible at high tide, the caves and natural bridge in Salsbury Cove in Bar Harbor were once thought to be an entrance to the underworld. In an imaginative stroke of geographic irony, one cave was later renamed Cathedral Rock. Located on private property but accessible by sea at low tide.

The Devil's Ovens rock formation along the shore in Bar Harbor is among the dozens of places in Maine associated with names Devil and Hell. *From Author's Collection.*

Maine Atlas: M16, A3

Devil's Pulpit, York

Not to be outdone by other towns whose promotional efforts went to "hell," the Ogunquit/York area sported more than one unholy natural attraction. They include York's Devil's Pulpit, a unique rock "throne" along the shore near Bald Head Cliff, as well as Devil's Kitchen, a deep notch in the ocean-side rocks along Marginal Way, Ogunquit's 1.25-mile shore walkway.

Maine Atlas: M1, A5

Hell's Gate, Bath

Steamboat captains feared plying the narrow channel of the Sasanoa River, known for its sharp rocks, and fierce currents. This tidal passage that connects the Kennebec River with the Sheepscot, undoubtedly felt like they were in navigation hell. Blasting done by the US Army Corps of Engineers in the early 1900s significantly reduced the risk.

Maine Atlas: M6, C5

Devil's Den, Andover

Located along on Black Brook, just off Devil's Den Road, the scenic cascades, dark, cool canyons, and overhang caves are best explored during warmer weather. The site even has its own Facebook page.

Maine Atlas: M18, C4

Hell Before Breakfast Cove, Sysladobsis Lake

Long lost off official maps, this bay in Sysladobsis Lake was reportedly named for the famous last words of one Sam Hill who, while swimming out fully clothed to retrieve a loose barge filled with bark for the local tannery, yelled back to shore "I'll fetch back that boat or go to hell before breakfast." He disappeared under the waves after observers said a mysterious dark shadow, rose from beneath the water.

Maine Atlas: M35, B2

Devil's Snowshoe Track, Milo

Storytellers share that Satan and his dog were fleeing Milo on a cold winter's night and left their tracks while trekking over a hillside ledge. The Devil supposedly sought shelter by blasting a cave with one fiery breath. Purportedly workers building a local dam on the nearby Sebec River around 1906 discovered similar tracks heading toward the cave.

Maine Atlas: M32, B4

Other places to go to the devil in Maine

Hell's Rapids, Kinney Nation	M45, C4
Devil's Half Acre, Bar Harbor	M16, B4
Hell's Half Acre Island, Stonington	M15, E4
Devil's Island, off Stonington	M15, E4
Devil's Footprint, Readfield	M12, B4
Devil's Back Trail, Harpswell	M6, D3
Devil's Bog, Skowhegan	M21, B1

A tourist keeps an eye out for Old Beelzebub while sitting in the Devil's Pulpit at Bald Head Cliff in York. *From Author's Collection.*

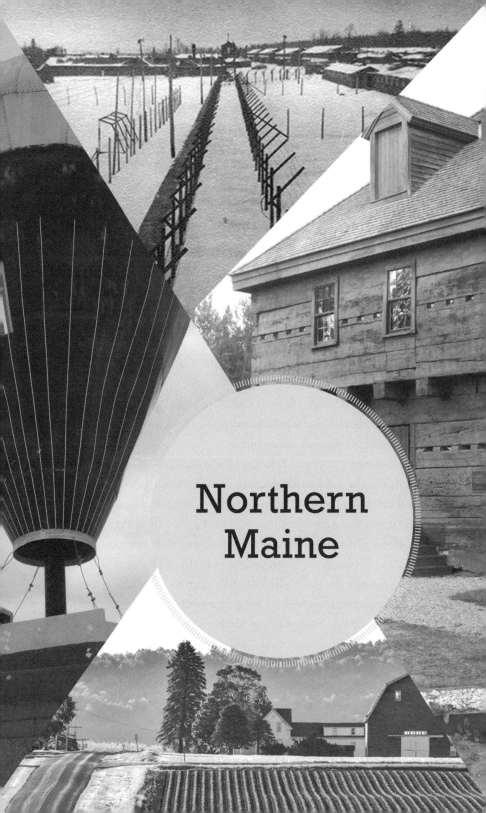

Northern
Maine

Northern Maine

When it comes to geography and culture, there are really three Maines. There is the coastal, inland, Northern—where life is as much about the journey as the destination.

In a state with sixteen counties, most of the north is comprised of just one, Aroostook—which is passionately called by its residents, and appropriately so, "The County." Covering more than 4.2 million acres, it is nearly as big as the next two largest counties combined. Along with pastoral sweeping potato fields, it is home to the St. John Valley where Acadian French heritage is still celebrated.

The centerpiece of the region is Katahdin, the highest peak in Maine at 5,267 feet. Katahdin, the northern terminus of the 2,200-mile long Appalachian Trail, is at a stout cairn making it exactly a mile high at the summit.

Nearby is Katahdin Woods and Waters National Monument and to the northeast lies the pristine Allagash Wilderness Waterway, one of the nation's premier canoe routes.

US Route 1 begins in Fort Kent and runs 2,369 miles south to Key West, Florida. And if that distance doesn't seem long enough, there's an actual scale model of our solar system (the largest such model in the world) that runs forty miles along the road from Presque Isle to Houlton. Drive it in an hour or less and you can brag about traveling at (scale) five times the speed of light! A flight of a different sort began in Presque Isle in 1978 when the first team to successfully cross the Atlantic in a balloon took off from Double Eagle Park.

A former sprawling Loring Air Force Base in Limestone, once home to nuclear weapons, has come a long way, it even hosted the band Phish's "Great Went," a Gen-X Woodstock that attracted 75,000.

From Fort Fairfield's annual Potato Blossom Festival, to agricultural fairs, to Fort Kent's Ploye Festival, there's always something interesting to do in The County.

Opposite (clockwise from top): A German POW Camp in Houlton (*Courtesy of Digicommons*); Fort Kent Blockhouse (*Courtesy of Digicommons*); Aroostook County potato field (*Courtesy of Paul Cyr*); Double Eagle II Balloon Launch Monument in Presque Isle (*From Author's Collection*).

Really Getting Away from it All

In a state famous for the expression "You can't get there from here," popularized in the late Marshall Dodge's "Bert and I" comedy albums, there is no shortage of remote locations.

A pair of Florida biologists, Ralph and Rebecca Means, however, have calculated the most remote spot in each state, based primarily on distance from any kind of road. The winner in Maine is a spot in the forest about a mile west of the Russell Pond Campground in the center of Baxter State Park.

As the crow flies it is more than six miles from any passable road, and in this case on the far side of some pretty big mountains. The only way to access the area is on foot, requiring hikes of more than ten miles, one way. To camp anywhere near it you must get a reservation, usually months in advance.

This area, the remote valley of the Wassataquoik, once teemed with logging activity. There were small towns, lumber camps, driving dams, and even a seven-hundred-foot sluice for sliding logs down mountainsides. All that has long since decayed to dust. Now, this is among the quietest places in Maine. Nearby is Wassataquoik Lake and picturesque Green Falls. Katahdin is six miles to the south.

The exact coordinates haven't been released, but rest assured, if you hike the trail from Russell Pond to Wassataquoik Lake, you're closer to being in the most remote spot in Maine than anyone else! *Maine Atlas: M50, B5*

Waging War Without a Shot

That's exactly what happened in 1838 when Maine and Canada came to blows in what is now called "The Bloodless Aroostook War." Soon after Maine became its own state in 1820, concerns began to grow about the exact location of the boundary with New Brunswick. Tensions escalated as loggers on each side of the current border cut timber on the other's territory and equipment was confiscated or destroyed.

Eventually, militias were called up, troops and cannons were positioned, forts were built in Fort Kent and Fort Fairfield, and muskets were kept on hair-trigger alert. Today, the media might have dubbed it "The Canadian Musket Crisis." While it never involved actual combat by large units, small, unsanctioned raids by groups of civilians continued into 1839.

The (Daniel) Webster-(Lord) Ashburton Treaty of 1842 finally established a permanent border and provided for the eventual creation of a Canadian rail line across the state.

During the war, human suffering was remarkably light. Three British soldiers were held captive for a time and two others were injured when attacked by a Maine black bear.

Maine recorded just one related death—Pvt. Hiram Smith, who reportedly died of some unrecorded calamity in 1828 while building "The Military Road" in the Haynesville area. Because the armies mostly just sat around and ate, the conflict is also known as the "Pork and Beans War." *Maine Atlas: M67, C4*

Presidential 'Fake News' Circa 1912

One of the more notable photographs of presidential candidate Teddy Roosevelt shows him astride a bull moose swimming across a lake. Roosevelt, of course, was no stranger to Maine, visiting numerous times as a boy and as an adult. Along with stops in major towns, Roosevelt toured Moosehead Lake, climbed Katahdin, and once visited friends at Schooner Head in Bar Harbor.

Most often though, Roosevelt spent time in Aroostook County, in the town of Island Falls where he went on guided hunts with Bill Sewall and Wilmot Dow. Roosevelt also was guided by Maine's first Registered Maine Guide, "Fly Rod" Crosby. Sewall and Dow went on to later run the future President's Elkhorn Ranch in North Dakota in 1884. The Sewall House in Island Falls is now a yoga retreat center.

Road's Toll Immortalized in Song

When a stretch of highway is immortalized by a hit song with the title "A Tombstone Every Mile," you know it's a special place. Route 2A, where it passes through the legendary Haynesville Woods, is the subject of country song written by Dan Fulkerson and recorded by Fort Fairfield's Dick Curless, a former trucker himself, back in 1965. The song was a smash hit, remaining on the charts for seventeen weeks, including two weeks at number five. It became the signature song for the eyepatch-wearing Curless whose son-in-law, the late Emmy-winning bluesman and rocker Bill Chinnock, of Yarmouth, continued the family musical tradition.

"Tombstone" was written in recognition of what was literally twenty miles of really bad road that resulted in many fatal car and truck crashes, particularly at a hairpin turn section.

If dead truckers every mile isn't enough to qualify this place as spooky, there's also a legend that a ghostly image of a young woman who died in a car crash also appears from time to time. The visible spirit of a young child, supposedly killed after being hit by a trailer truck, has also been reported.

Oh, and that swimming moose photo? It is an excellent example of early photo manipulation—it was fabricated by a New York newspaper using pictures of a swimming moose and Roosevelt riding a horse. Roosevelt at the time was running for president under the banner of the Bull Moose Party.

Maine Atlas: M52, B3

A manipulated photo that shows President Theodore Roosevelt "riding" a moose.
Courtesy of Digicommons.

A pair of rusting locomotives located along the remote Allagash River in Northern Maine. *Courtesy of Ron Beard.*

Also, along Route 2A is the grave of Hiram Smith, the only man to die in the "Bloodless War" with Canada in 1828 *(See page 84)*. His original stone on the east side of the road, north of "town" was stolen, but replaced in the 1980s with one that erroneously states he was killed in the "Indian Wars."

Either way, it's impossible to drive this road without the lyrics of Curless' song popping into your head: "If they'd buried all them truckers lost in them woods, there'd be a tombstone every mile." *Maine Atlas: M53, D1*

Rusting Relics Recall Railway

Perhaps no place provides a more iconic and poignant snapshot of the former industrialized nature of the North Woods in Maine than the rusting steam locomotives along the Allagash Wilderness Waterway.

Needing far more horsepower than draft animals and Lombard Loaders could provide alone, crews in the winter of 1926-1927 hauled tons of rail, freight car parts, and entire locomotives into the deep

Maine woods from Quebec. Supplies were ferried in from the opposite direction from Greenville.

The result was the Umbazookus and Eagle Lake Railroad, later known as the Eagle Lake and West Branch Railroad. The thirteen-mile line featured a 1,500-foot trestle across the north end of Chamberlain Lake. When the railroad was abandoned in 1933, after carrying an estimated million cords of wood, the steam locomotives remained in a shed between Chamberlain and Eagle lakes. That shed accidentally burned in 1969, exposing the locomotives. In later years, vandals stripped some parts off the engines.

Crews of volunteers from the Allagash Alliance have since stabilized the units, removed hazardous materials, placed them back on sections of rail and protected them. If not by canoe on the Eagle Lake side, the easiest way to visit the locomotives is by snowmobile. *Maine Atlas: M55, D5*

Aliens and Abduction Along the Allagash

The US Air Force's Project Blue Book may have wrapped up six years earlier, but the UFO (Unidentified Flying Object) phenomena got a shot in the arm in 1976 following reports of flying saucers, complete with an abduction by aliens, along the Allagash Wilderness Waterway.

Accounts at the time claim that twin brothers Jim Weiner and Jack Weiner, and friends Charles Foltz and Charles Rak, all students from Massachusetts, were camping on the shores of Eagle Lake when they saw unexplained, fast-moving lights in the sky. Four-fingered alien "Grays" with almond-shaped eyes aboard the craft reportedly "probed" the men and conducted tests. The men reported the UFOs to a ranger immediately, but the reported abductions were only revealed when memories resurfaced during hypnosis sessions.

The abduction incident received widespread media attention, was profiled in a book, and was the subject of an episode of the TV show *Unsolved Mysteries*.

Walt Disney feeds a fawn from Maine used as a model for animators working on the movie "Bambi." *Courtesy of Walt Disney Studios.*

So, was it really aliens intent on some good brook trout fishing, or were the lights merely secret military aircraft known to frequent the skies over Northern Maine? The jury is still out.

The *St. John Valley Times* ran a story in 2016 in which one of the men, Chuck Rak, recanted, claiming that some recreational drugs were used on the canoe trip and that he went along with the others for "financial gain." The same story reports that Foltz, who sticks by the abduction narrative, said the men had only consumed one beer each when departing Telos Landing. *Maine Atlas: M55, D5*

Disney's Bambi Inspired by Baxter

Few people realize while watching Walt Disney's classic, "Bambi," that Baxter State Park served as the inspiration for the setting. Damariscotta artist, sculptor, photographer and avid outdoorsman Maurice "Jake" Day was working as an animator for Disney in California when he convinced Walt that Bambi should be a white-tailed deer, rather than a western mule deer. In the book, Bambi was a European roe deer. He arranged to send two orphaned Maine deer, dubbed Bambi and Faline, to the studios to serve as models.

Disney later sent Day, who was named by Gov. Percival Baxter as the park's official Artist in Residence, and another artist to the park where they spent weeks photographing the scenery, which inspired the art of the film. Day was a frequent park visitor before his stint in California. He was the head of a group of friends who frequently explored the park together. Eventually they became known as "Jake's Rangers." Among those who tagged along on some of those excursions were Supreme Court Justice William O. Douglas. At age 78, Day, wearing moccasins, climbed Katahdin with Maine Gov. Kenneth Curtis. *Maine Atlas: M7, A3*

Town Celebrates Going to Dogs

With the requisite snow, ice, backcountry, and wilderness spirit, Fort Kent is the perfect place for Maine's answer to the venerable Iditarod sled dog race in Alaska. Every March, nearly a hundred teams of dog and their owners and support crews descend on Fort Kent for the Can-Am Crown International Sled Dog Race. It features courses of 30, 60, and 250 miles, the later serving as a qualifying race for the Iditarod. Entrants compete for thousands of dollars in prize money. The total purse in 2020, the race's twenty-eighth year, was $43,000. Scores of area residents take mushers into their homes and hundreds of volunteers help make the event happen.

The two shorter races are usually completed in a single day. The longer one involves a series of checkpoints and mandatory rest breaks and can take two to four days. All mushers begin their respective races on Main Street in Fort Kent where snow is hauled in to cover the pave-

A sled dog team heads out of Fort Kent during the annual Can-Am Crown International Sled Dog Race.
Courtesy of Paul Cyr.

ment, if necessary. Hundreds of people gather at the starting line to cheer on the world-class mushers and their dogs. *Maine Atlas: M67, C4*

Some Enchanted Hole in the Earth

Most caves in Maine are relatively small in size and are little more than gaps and passages among fallen boulders (Talus caves) or places where the action of the sea has eroded softer rock sandwiched between harder upper and lower layers (Sea caves).

While there are ice caves, there are no really large water-eroded caverns like those found in other states. One of the most accessible is Enchanted Cave, located in a band of limestone south of Jackman. Stretching for about 450 feet, Enchanted Cave is the longest, although not the deepest, in the state.

Home to frogs and salamanders, the cave features rocks that do show signs of being smoothed and shaped by water although it lacks any large stalagmites or stalactites.

The caves, also known as McKenney Caves, are located on private property and Maine has a Cave Protection Act that prohibits folks from damaging or vandalizing any cave. Guided tours can be arranged by the folks at the nearby Bulldog Camps on Enchanted Pond. They advise: Bring your own headlamp, clothes for crawling through mud, and plan on getting wet. *Maine Atlas: M39, D5*

Treaty Split Town, Houses, in Two

Lots of people like to think of themselves as having feet in multiple worlds, but at the border crossing between the US and Canada at Estcourt Station, that is entirely possible.

When the border between the two countries was finally settled in 1842, the line drawn on the map by negotiators in Washington, D.C., ran straight through the tiny village, even through some houses, in the far, northwest corner of Maine. Although no one currently lives on the Maine side year-round, a small US Customs Border Checkpoint is staffed most days to allow for loggers and others to cross.

For decades, the border for people living there was not an inconvenience. However, after the increase in security following the 9/11

The remote village of Estcourt Station is divided by the border between the US and Canada. *Courtesy of Wikicommons.*

terrorist attacks, everything changed. In 2002, two Canadian men were arrested and detained for days in separate incidents for crossing the border without checking in. Their reason: They just wanted to buy gasoline at a station on the American side where fuel was much cheaper. The gas station too eventually closed.

As for those houses split by the border, US Customs treats them as being entirely in the Canadian village of Pohenegamook. As one agent is quoted as saying in *Down East* Magazine, "We're not going to have you come check in with us when you go to the bathroom in a back room that's in the United States." *Maine Atlas: M67, see inset*

Barrel-themed Tree Inspires Fun

Mainers can be quite inventive when it comes to finding new ways to decorate for Christmas. After all, in a state that is ninety percent forested, putting lights on another tree is the festive equivalent of the same old, same old.

Along the coast, public installations run toward the nautical with "trees" made up of lobster traps and lobster cars. In Fort Fairfield, however, in the heart of potato-growing country, it's potato barrels that get the call. That town's tree is located on Main Street, adjacent to the Old Blockhouse Fort and Museum decorated by volunteers with the Fort Fairfield Quality of Place Council.

Standing five barrels high, it is decorated with a continuous garland and large red bows and topped by a star outline created with lights. At other times of year, it is decorated with seasonal themes, such as US flags on the Fourth of July.

When it comes to celebrating potatoes, Fort Fairfield goes all in. They also hold an annual Potato Blossom Festival, which is spread over nine days and features more than one hundred events, including a parade, fireworks, car show, townwide yard sale, and crowning of a Potato Blossom Queen. *Maine Atlas: M65, C4*

Stream Flows Both Ways Near Imaginary Town

It's marked on the map, but there's really no there, there. The bridge over the West Branch of the Penobscot River on the storied ninety-six-mile Golden Road opened up hundreds of thousands of acres of timber to harvesters in the early 1970s.

Marked as "Hannibal's Crossing" on maps with a font and type size indicating a large community, there never was a ferry crossing or town there. It seems television weatherman, Lew Colby, of WCSH, in Portland, often gave current conditions for "Hannibal's Crossing," which is a fictitious village he created in good fun. A black fly index was sometimes included.

Reportedly, the bridge itself was named "Hannibal's Crossing," after the Great Northern Paper Company crews that built it, no doubt familiar with Colby's forecasts, compared the feat to the celebrated elephant-loving general's crossing of the Alps on the way to sack Rome in 218 BC. For many years, a bootleg sign at the bridge declared the name.

Nearby is Lobster Stream, which drains a lake of the same name

When it was competed in the 1960s, the Golden Road north of the paper mills in Millinocket was considered an engineering marvel. *Courtesy of Millinocket Historical Society.*

and is a tributary of the West Branch. Depending on the time of year, water flows from the stream into the river, or out of the river and up into the lake. Remember, logging trucks, not private vehicles, have right of way on this private road. Access to explore the waters is best from the state boat launch ramp on Lobster Stream. *Maine Atlas: M49, D3*

Maine's Tallest Mountain by Any Name

At exactly 5,267 feet tall, Baxter Peak on Katahdin is the undisputed high point of Maine. At one point in the past, realizing it was only thirteen feet shy of a mile, enterprising visitors constructed a tall thin cairn of rocks so it could be called "Mile-High" Katahdin but the current stack is not that big. Katahdin remains the heart of Baxter State Park, created by the efforts and philanthropy of former Gov. Percival Baxter.

Debate still rages on whether or not the mountain should be called "Mount Katahdin," or merely "Katahdin." Where Katahdin in Abenaki means "Greatest Mountain," purists argue it is obviously redundant to call it, in effect, "Mount Greatest Mountain." But Mount Katahdin has a nice ring to it.

Along with being a destination on any serious hiker's bucket list, the summit is the official Northern Terminus of the storied Appalachian Trail which stretches 2,200 miles from Georgia to Maine. The trail was originally planned to end atop Mount Washington in New Hampshire, but conservation hero Myron Avery of Lubec convinced Benton MacKaye to extend the footpath to Katahdin.

While many people have climbed Katahdin multiple times, the unofficial record undoubtedly goes to early Baxter Ranger LeRoy Dudley who is estimated to have hiked to the top from Chimney Pond five hundred times. *Maine Atlas: M50, D5*

Precipitous Trail Requires Razor Focus

In the pantheon of tough hiking trails in Maine, which includes the Precipice in Acadia, Mahoosuc Notch and the 100 Miles on the Appalachian Trail, and Gulf Hagas, The Knife Edge on Katahdin stands above them all.

Similar to others that are described as more of a "non-technical climbing route" than a trail, The Knife Edge is literally only a few feet wide in places with drops of hundreds of feet on either side. That's a razor-thin margin of safety in anyone's book.

The actual trail is a 1.1-mile scramble from Baxter Peak, east across South Peak, to where the trail really narrows, and then over to Pamola Peak. A total loop including the "Edge," requires nearly ten miles of hiking. Even in places where it appears the slopes are gradual, tall, impassable cliffs lurk below. In one section, a rounded, two-foot wide, section of rock ten feet high, merely has a trail blaze painted halfway up, leaving hikers to decide the best way around.

More than fifty people have died on the mountain. Rangers advise against ever attempting The Knife Edge or any Katahdin trail in poor weather. Your destination is a safe return to the trailhead, not the top of the mountain they warn. *Maine Atlas: M51, D1*

'Woods And Waters' are Monument to Katahdin

The impressive list of parks and preserves in Maine got a little longer in 2016 with the creation of the Katahdin Woods and Waters National Monument on more than 87,000 acres—valued at $60 million—east of Baxter State Park.

The parcels, which include frontage on many pristine lakes and along the East Branch of the Penobscot River, were donated by Roxanne Quimby, the founder of the natural products company Burt's Bees. Quimby and her son, Lucas St. Clair, run the Elliotsville Plantation and Quimby Family Foundation, which have also conserved lands abutting numerous other parks and preserves in the state.

Operating from a small office in Millinocket, and a visitor contact center in Patten, the monument has slowly been developed to include hiking trails, picnic areas, and campsites along with an eighteen-mile gravel "Loop Road" that includes spectacular vistas of Katahdin in Baxter State Park.

The International Appalachian Trail (IAT) passes through the monument along the many waterfalls and cascades of the East Branch. In winter, cross country ski trails are open, including in the upper East Branch area at the Matagamon entrance where there are twenty-five miles of groomed ski trails along with a series of warming huts.

During his time in office, Maine Governor Paul LePage prohibited direction signs to the new monument from being erected on state land. After he left office, in January 2019, that policy was reversed. *Maine Atlas: M51, A2*

Debsconeag Caves Lure Cool Customers

While Maine may lack impressive caverns such as Carlsbad or Mammoth caverns, it does have another subterranean geologic feature that's as cool as it comes. Several places in Maine sport what are referred to as "ice caves," usually deep openings and voids below north-facing boulder fields where water freezes in winter and sometimes doesn't even melt by high summer.

Pamola Caves at Baxter State Park, Moose Cave in Mahoosuc Notch and caves at Allagash Lake along the Wilderness Waterway, often have long-lingering ice. But perhaps the easiest to access, and most impressive, are the caves in The Nature Conservancy's Debsconeag Lakes Wilderness located off the Golden Road, northwest of Millinocket.

Here, iron rungs installed in the boulders help get you safely into the cool, damp confines well below ground level in the deep, mossy forest. In the 1950s, people staying in nearby camps often tapped the ice in the caves to keep food and beverages cold.

The name Debsconeag, which means "carrying place," is rooted in Native American canoe routes that took advantage of the many lakes and ponds in the area. *Maine Atlas: M50, E5*

When Prisoners and Potatoes Went Hand-in-Hand

With its remote, rural scenery, unforgiving climate, and rugged terrain, Maine was seen as the perfect place to put camps for German prisoners in World War II. Along with a camp near Spencer Lake in Jackman, there were others in Princeton and in Houlton. Half a dozen smaller satellite camps were also spread around the state.

The Houlton complex opened in the fall of 1944 at the former Houlton Army Air Base. It was later renamed Camp Houlton, which operated until the spring of 1946. It was capable of housing two thousand prisoners, but most times had only 1,100. It was the largest in

German prisoners of war were able to keep busy, and make money for goods from the camp canteen, by working in Aroostook County potato fields. *Courtesy of Digicommons.*

Maine by far. It included a double fence line, multiple rows of long, narrow barracks, a mess hall, guard towers, and other buildings.

Considering the conditions prisoners might have faced on various European battlefronts, the camp was not a hardship. Many prisoners were allowed to work in local potato fields and used the $1 per day "script" they earned to buy cigarettes and other items in the camp's spacious exchange. The prisoners also cut timber and built bridges.

One man later married the daughter of a farmer he had worked for in Sherman while a prisoner. The former POW camp is now the Houlton Airport. There is a marker on the site. *Maine Atlas: M53, A4*

Snowmobile on Steroids Had Track in Back

While railroads had been using steam power for three-quarters of a century, it wasn't until 1901 that Waterville blacksmith and inventor Alvin Orlando Lombard patented and began building steam-powered tracked vehicles to haul timber from the woods. The first Lombard Log Hauler was christened "Mary Anne."

Between 1901 and 1918 Lombard built more than eighty of the devices that looked like locomotives without wheels. They featured tracks on the rear and steerable skis or small iron wheels on the front. Described today as "30-ton snowmobiles," Lombard's haulers produced about fifty horsepower and had a top speed of just under five miles per hour. They could move three hundred tons of wood at a time. To operate the hauler took a crew of three—an engineer, a fireman, and a third poor soul who sat exposed on the front and attempted to steer.

Still, they could haul multiple strings of sleds filled with logs which was a vast improvement over horses or oxen. The record length for a single train was more than a quarter mile. Lombard also designed and built a line of smaller, yet still massive, gasoline tractor trucks.

Along with Maine, other states where Lombard haulers were used included Michigan, Wisconsin, and New Hampshire. A Lombard

A logging crew at Jordan's Mill at Grindstone poses with their high-tech Lombard Loader while a visitor sits up front in the steering position.
Courtesy of Digicommons.

steam hauler is on exhibit outside the Patten Lumberman's Museum. The Maine Forest and Logging Museum in Bradley has two working Lombards in its collection. *Maine Atlas: M23, A4*

Dedicated Riders Need Diehard Derrieres

With bragging rights as the first of its type dedicated to long distance motorcycling, Madawaska's Four Corners Park has become a true international destination. It is located on a hillside terrace overlooking the main drag downtown and was created for those hearty souls seeking to ride to, and connect with, the outmost corners of the continental United States. The other spots are Blaine, Washington; San Ysidro, California; and Key West in Florida.

The Four Corners Challenge to reach those spots in just twenty-one days was created by the Southern California Motorcycle Association. The idea for the park came from local rider Joe LaChance after he and his wife, Diane, completed the challenge in 2000. Area businesses, contractors, and volunteers made it happen.

As the only one of the cardinal points of motorcycling to feature a park, Maine's entry includes a fountain and a twelve-foot granite monument "dedicated to those wind-burnt and saddle-sore participants," who seek to complete the challenge. There's also a rest room and information center. Riders who finish are eligible to have their names carved into brick paving stones.

LaChance has created a "Titanium" Four Corners Tour within Maine with stops in Madawaska, Grafton Notch, Kittery, and Lubec. Upon completion of four circuits (no time limit) riders have their names enshrined online and are automatically qualified to receive and wear the illustrious "Titanium Butt Club" t-shirt and pin.
Maine Atlas: M68, A3

Lake is a Monument to Ingenuity

In 1834, just over a dozen years after Maine became a state, woodsman, surveyor, and engineer Shepard Boody stood on the shore of Telos Lake in far northern Maine and saw not just a place from which expeditions to all the state's major river systems could be launched, but fortune and fame.

Prior to that time, timber from five hundred square miles in the Allagash area was driven north, to the St. John River, where its owners were required to pay Canadian duty. Boody built a dam on Chamberlain Lake to raise the water twenty feet blending it with Telos. Another dam at the east end of Telos, and creation of a canal in an ancient stream bed, reversed the flow sending a torrent of water, wood, and the wealth it represented into the East Branch of the Penobscot River, and to the mills of Bangor.

Telos, which in Greek means end or purpose, is also the nexus of many canoe routes in Maine. From that lake, adventurers can paddle the Allagash and St. John and, with portages of no more than a mile or two, to such places as Mud Pond and Umbazookus, Chesuncook, and Moosehead lakes, and access the Kennebec and the Penobscot river watersheds. The Northern Forest Canoe Trail passes nearby.

A dispute between the Telos Dam's owners and timber barons irked by a toll to send logs over the spillway sparked the so-called "Telos War" in the mid-1800s. A group of two dozen river drivers with pick poles and axes were confronted by more than fifty similarly armed ruffians imported from Bangor for security at the dam. No blows were exchanged and reports indicate things were settled over copious mugs of rum. *Maine Atlas: M50, A3*

Fort Kent is Place of Beginnings

All great journeys have a beginning and an end and for those seeking to drive the entire 2,369 miles of US Route 1, the northernmost of the nation's north-south highways, the place to start is in Fort Kent. It is the longest such route in the US.

A sign at the end of the bridge between Fort Kent and Clair, New Brunswick, declares the start of the road that reaches all the way to

The beginning of US Route 1 in Fort Kent is billed as America's First Mile.
Courtesy of Paul Cyr.

Key West, Florida, where, interestingly enough, a sign declares it is the start of US Route 1. Of course, they are both right as one is the start of US Route 1 South and the other US Route 1 North.

In Maine, US Route 1 heads south down the east side of the state from Fort Kent, passing through Presque Isle, Houlton, and Calais before hugging the coast due west through Ellsworth and communities along the midcoast, through Portland, eventually leaving the state in Kittery.

The first such route was established in 1911. In 1915, the official northern terminus of the "Atlantic Highway," was in Calais. In 1925, the Joint Committee on Interstate Highways designated the official US Route 1, although the exact path has shifted slightly over the years. It originally ran inland through Bangor, but was shifted to the Down East coast after the Hancock-Waldo Bridge, a long-span

Painted Rock. *From Author's Collection.*

Wonderful!

Picture Place

While spray paint on roadside rocks in Maine is usually considered to be unwelcome graffiti, the one exception is Painted Rock on the main access route to Baxter State Park and Katahdin. The glacial erratic is considered the largest formally painted boulder in New England.

Located on a long straight stretch of road where lofty Katahdin looms tall in the background, Painted Rock admonishes passersby to "Keep Maine Beautiful." It was painted by Maine Youth Conservation Corps campers in 1979.

It has become one of the most photographed spots in that area appearing in thousands of "selfies." It is was known originally as Pockwockamus Rock after nearby Pockwockamus Stream and Pond. Pockwockamus is believed to mean "little muddy pond."

For more than two decades, Abbott and Nancy Meader of Oakland helped maintain and occasionally repaint the rock. They retired from those duties in 2013, according to the *Bangor Daily News.*

Maine Atlas: M51, E1

suspension bridge that opened in 1931. The old route through Bangor was redesignated as US Route 1A.

In all, there are 526 miles of US Route 1 in Maine. There is also a designated US Bicycle Route 1 in Maine. In Washington County, the two share some of the same roads. *Maine Atlas: M67, C4*

Lost Boy Later Found Home in Maine

The nation held its collective breath for nine days in July 1939 as hundreds of volunteers searched the woods, boulder caves, and windswept summits of Baxter State Park for a lost 12-year-old Boy Scout from New York.

Donn Fendler, who shared his ordeal in the book, *Lost on a Mountain in Maine*, got separated from his hiking party during a storm on the wide, open Tableland just below the summit of Katahdin. Hundreds of volunteers along with park rangers, game wardens, and police combed the park looking for any sign of him.

Eventually, Fendler stumbled out of the woods near an occupied cabin at the confluence of Wassataquoik Stream and the East Branch of the Penobscot River, some thirty-five miles from where he had been last seen. He was dirty, naked, barefoot, and covered with bug bites. He was seriously dehydrated and had lost sixteen pounds. He credited his scout skills and training to "follow a stream downhill," for getting him out alive.

His survival was front-page news around the country and was covered by *Life Magazine*. In 1939, President Franklin D. Roosevelt presented him with the Army and Navy Legion of Valor medal for being a youth hero. Fendler, who went on to become an Army Green Beret, later spent summers in Newport, Maine. In 2014, July 25 was declared Donn Fendler Day by Gov. Paul LePage. Fendler died in 2016 at age 90. *Maine Atlas: M51,D4*

Saw Museum is a Cut Above

Perhaps more than any other tool for working in the woods, the chain saw helped sustain the timber industry in Maine after it was widely adopted in the 1920s. Prior its use, trees were felled by teams of lumberjacks using axes and long, steel crosscut blades with handles on both ends for two people.

The earliest chain saws were heavy and unwieldy and also required two people to operate. The history of chainsaws, particularly in the St. John Valley, is lovingly preserved in the Louie's Antique Chain Saws museum in the village of Allagash.

Run by Louis Pelletier, the institution now houses more than four hundred chain saws. But more than a mere repository of artifacts, the museum also strives to preserve the stories of the men, and women, who used those saws, lovingly cared for them, and made their livings in the North Maine Woods. There are saws specially designed for left-handed users, saws of every color, size, and configuration. Some were even mounted on wheels.

It's taken Pelletier more than forty years to put the collection together. Louis and his son run Allagash Wood Products which manufactures Adirondack chairs, picnic tables, and other wood products. *Maine Atlas: M66, E4*

Tarratine Marker Recalls Terrible Toll

Throughout the wilds of Maine can be found furtive attempts to memorialize people or events that loomed large in the lives of those who previously traveled those roads, those paths, those rivers. In most instances these plaques, engraved stones, or simple wooden markers commemorate major undertakings or well-known leaders. But some are meant to share the memory of calamity or the labors of those who toiled on the lower rungs of the social ladder.

Perhaps the most forlorn is the Tarratine Monument, located along the tracks of Canadian Pacific Railroad Line. About a mile west of the road crossing in the former village of Tarratine between Rockwood and Jackman sits a mysterious, broken, three-foot tall obelisk inscribed with the letters RAM and 1888. That is the year when railroad construction crews were rushing to complete the line.

Near the base are the words "Sons of Italy."

Historian Walter MacDougall, as well as folks involved in restoring the Old Railroad Depot in Greenville, believe it memorializes Italian quarry men (some say three men died, others say six, still others believe thirteen) who were killed when dynamite they were using for a rock cut nearby detonated prematurely.

Basic laborers, especially immigrants, were considered expendable in those days. No newspaper accounts of the accident can be found. There would not have been an investigation. Most likely the men were quickly buried near where they died, and work resumed. Some fellow crew members were believed to have erected the stone. What the letters RAM stand for remains a mystery. Because of the Masonic symbolism suggested by the style of the letter "A" they may have been Royal Arch Masons, which was not unusual for Italian stonecutters during that time. *Maine Atlas: M40, B4*

The *Double Eagle II* Has Launched, and Landed

Lifting off from an Aroostook County potato field, three Americans became the first people to successfully cross the Atlantic Ocean in a helium-filled balloon. Ben Abruzzo, Maxie Anderson, and pilot Larry Newman crammed into a gondola that measured only 15 by 7.5 by 4.5 feet. Attached to the bottom was a hang-glider that the men never got to use. It had to be jettisoned over the ocean as ballast.

The *Double Eagle II* rose into the skies at 8:43 p.m. on August 11, 1978. It landed 137 hours and six minutes later in a field north of

Paris, France. Two of the men had failed a year earlier in a flight that originated in Massachusetts. Two previous unsucessful attempts by other teams had launched from Bar Harbor.

In 1984, Joe Kittinger successfully completed the first solo translantic balloon flight, launching from Caribou. While in France, Newman enjoyed the honor of sleeping in the same bed in the US Embassy used by aviator Charles Lindbergh after his first successful solo

Go Way Far Out in 'The County'

There are lots of places in Maine that are out of this world, but Aroostook County takes it to the extreme. For nearly forty miles along Route 1 you can drive through a 3D scale model of our solar system. It is the largest of its kind in the Western Hemisphere—second largest in the world.

Running from a fifty-foot yellow ring representing the sun at the Northern Maine Museum of Science at the University of Maine at Presque Isle to lowly Pluto, just an inch across, inside the visitor information center at Houlton it covers some 3,670,050,000 scale miles.

It takes more than five hours for light from the actual sun to reach Pluto, but you can cover that same distance in scale in less than one hour without breaking any speed limits or the laws of physics.

The Maine Solar System model is the brainchild of Kevin McCartney, a professor at the University of Maine at Presque Isle, who coordinated the project. It took several years for volunteers to construct and install all the pieces with local technical schools and high schools building the planets, moons, and bases with the backing of service organizations. It was dedicated in 2003.

The largest planets, including Jupiter and Saturn, are between four and five feet in diameter. By comparison, Earth is just a puny 5.5 inches in diameter. Our moon, about sixteen feet away, is just 1.5 inches in diameter. In 2017, Jupiter "disappeared," for several months while it was in the shop to have its fiberglass shell refurbished.

Folks in Northern Maine also let the planets go to their heads each year when they celebrate "Planet Head Day." Participants shave their heads and then paint them to look like planets, raising money to fight cancer.

And Pluto? It is represented twice on the model. When the original was built Pluto was considered a planet. Its model was kept in a locked case indoors, crossing of the Atlantic in an airplane in 1927.

The *Double Eagle II* gondola is on display at the Smithsonian National Air and Space Museum in Washington, D.C. A special park and memorial to the feat is located on the Spragueville Road, south of Presque Isle. The County celebrates its ballooning heritage each year with the Crown of Maine Balloon Festival. *Maine Atlas: M65, E1*

reportedly because people kept stealing it. The location represents its average distance from the sun. After Pluto was downgraded to "dwarf planet" in 2006, it and two other dwarfs were installed at its then distance from the sun, which is only thirty-three miles from Presque Isle.

Models of other dwarf planets are even farther out, including Eris, some fifty-four miles south of Houlton, and in Canada.

Fastest Man in the Universe

When NASA's New Horizons spacecraft beamed back the first close-up photos from Pluto in July 2015, marathoner, teacher, and coach Evan Graves of Caribou was tapped to celebrate the transmission of those images back to Earth by running non-stop along the solar system model from Pluto in Houlton to Presque Isle carrying a thumb drive of planetary photos. More than sixty other runners joined him for part of the way. He covered the more than thirty-nine miles in a time equivalent to traveling at the model's scale speed of light, some 186,282 miles a second!

Above right: A man with a planet head. *Courtesy of David Allen.* Right: A truck lifting Jupiter into place. *Courtesy of University of Maine at Presque Isle.*

Mars Hill Robber Captured Public's Attention

Bank robber Bernard Patterson walked into the Northern National Bank in Mars Hill on November 12, 1971, wearing a trench coat, sunglasses, and a bright blue wig. The 24-year-old walked out and into the history books with more than $110,000 in cash—nearly $750,000 today—setting a record for the largest robbery in Maine.

Escaping down a local stream using an inflatable raft, the decorated Vietnam veteran, was skilled at living in the rough. He hid out on nearby Mars Hill Mountain for several days before fleeing after learning one of the tellers had recognized him and that the largest manhunt in the state's history might be closing in.

During the next seven months, Maine's most famous fugitive traveled across the country, rode a motorcycle across Europe, and even went to North Africa where he reportedly purchased a camel and got lost in the desert. Along the way he exhibited a fondness for wine, women, and generosity toward those in need. The exploits of plane hijacker D.B. Cooper, just a few weeks after the robbery, helped knock the story off front pages.

As profiled in the book *The Great Mars Hill Bank Robbery*, by Ron Chase, Patterson, nearly out of money and tired of running, turned himself in at Scotland Yard in London. He was extradited to the United States, was convicted, and served time in prison.

After returning to The County, Patterson worked at various jobs, including running a medical marijuana grow operation. He died in 2003 at age 56. *Maine Atlas: M59, A3*

Baxter State Park

With the rooftop of Maine, Katahdin, as its centerpiece, Baxter State Park is the heart and soul of the state's wilderness experience. That energy was well understood by the state's Native Americans who considered their "Greatest Mountain" sacred. That ancient force remains a powerful pull to tens of thousands of visitors to the 220,000-acre preserve to this day.

But along with natural features and occurrences mentioned elsewhere in these pages, evidence of other curiosities, abandoned human endeavors, logging operations, erstwhile settlements, and calamities await discovery by modern-day explorers throughout the park at places mentioned only cryptically in guidebooks and seldom marked on maps.

Fort Mountain Plane Crash

On June 20, 1944, the pristine silence of the thick forest on the slopes of Fort Mountain in the southern part of Baxter was shattered by the roaring engines and the tearing of metal as an off-course C-54 Skymaster cargo plane slammed into the ground near the summit. The crash and subsequent fire killed all six crew members and the sole passenger. It took recovery crews seven days to reach the site. There are no trails on Fort Mountain. *Maine Atlas: M50, C5*

Katahdin Arctic Butterfly

While Native Americans believed the summit of Katahdin was home only to the fearsome Pamola, God of Thunder, who had the head of a moose, torso of a man, and wings and talons of an eagle, its most unusual actual resident of the high alpine zone is the Katahdin Arctic Butterfly. With a wingspread of just one and a half inches, this endangered butterfly is found nowhere else on the planet. *Maine Atlas: M50, D5*

Opposite (clockwise from top): A C-54 military transport plane, similar to this one, crashed on remote Fort Mountain in Baxter State Park in 1944 (*Courtesy of Wikicommons*); A logging crew deep in the Wassataquoik region of Baxter Sate Park in the mid 1800s (*Courtesy of Digicommons*). The rare butterfly found at the summit of Mount Katahdin (*Courtesy of the University of Maine*).

Pamola Ice Caves

Located on the north side of Pamola Peak off the Dudley Trail, the Ice Caves were formed by the movement of a series of massive granite slabs. Their large, open spaces invite exploration (no flashlights needed) by humans who will no doubt wonder if the smooth, flat walls and ceilings are natural or man-made. Temperatures remain cool in the caves long into high summer. *Maine Atlas: M51, D1*

Dry Pond

The horseshoe-shaped Great Basin that contains Chimney Pond and the fabled Knife Edge headwall is also home to a unique body of water known as Dry Pond. Hikers heading toward the basin skirt the edge of this boulder-lined oddity. In spring, it can be full of water in the morning but dry by afternoon. Geologists theorize that it empties when winter ice lingering far below ground finally melts, allowing the water to drain away. *Maine Atlas: M51, C1*

Unknown River Driver Graves

Driving logs to market on the spring freshet on the streams and rivers of Northern Maine was always a dangerous job. Especially hazardous was breaking up logjams at falls and narrow places. Baxter State Park holds the graves of six Unknown River Drivers who were customarily buried where they died, their identities lost to history. One is located along the Park Tote Road, near Grand Pitch on Nesowadnehunk Stream. *Maine Atlas: M50, C4*

Caribou Reintroduction

Maine was once home to tens of thousands of Woodland Caribou, but they were hunted to extinction. The last sighting was atop Katahdin in 1908. An effort to reintroduce twenty-three Caribou from Canada onto the treeless Thoreau Tableland atop Katahdin in 1963 failed. A similar effort in 1993 involving twelve Caribou met the same fate as the animals wandered off or were killed by predators. *Maine Atlas: M50, D5*

Lost 'City' of the Wassataquoik

Despite Baxter State Park's mission of protecting the woods, waters and mountains as "forever wild," that has not always been the case. Many areas of the park, particularly its seldom-trekked interior, were once heavily logged. Rusting equipment, cellar holes, and iron relics can be spotted as nature subsumes the hand of humans in many places. Chief among them is New City, a once-thriving village in the Wassataquoik Valley, nearly nine miles in from the closest road. By the end of its four-year heyday the settlement included a school, church, and blacksmith shop. A short hike away is Inscription Rock, carved to commemorate the start of logging operations in 1883. *Maine Atlas: M51, C1*

Reintroducing the Caribou to Maine.
Courtesy of Maine Department of Inland Fisheries and Wildlife.

Maine's Number One!

Everyone knows that Maine is number one when it comes to the friendliest people around and the most spectacular scenery—on the East Coast anyway. But along with other geographical and socio-demographic superlatives, Maine is no slouch when it comes to making the pages of the world's number one publication of record holders—*The Guinness Book of World Records*. Additional details on many of these items can be found elsewhere in this book.

Maine In 3D

The University of Maine Advanced Structures and Composites Center in Orono set three *Guinness* records in October 2019 when it "printed" a seventy-three-foot boat named 3Dirigo out of composite material. The records include Largest 3D Printed Boat and Largest 3D Printed Object, using the world's Largest 3D Polymer Printer.

Most Simultaneous Moose Callers

Exactly 1,054 people set the record for the most simultaneous moose calls at the Maine Moose Festival in Skowhegan on June 9, 2018. The rules required they grunt, howl, and bellow for thirty seconds.

Largest Snowperson on Earth

On February 26, 2008, residents in Bethel used thirteen million pounds of snow to create a snowwoman measuring 122 feet, 1 inch tall.

Longest Snowmobile Journey

A trip of some 12,163 miles by snowmobile in January through March of 2008 was made by Robert G. Davis, on the trail networks in Canada and in Maine.

Most Corn Husked in One Minute

In 2015, Michael Diggins Jr. of Scarborough shucked thirteen ears of corn in one minute.

Longest Tap Dance

A team of thirteen tap students from the Centre of Movement School of Performing Arts tap-danced from Portland to Gorham in October 2002. It took four hours and 33 minutes.

First Helium Balloon to Cross the Atlantic

In August 1978, Maxie Anderson, Ben Abruzzo, and Larry Newman lifted off from Presque Isle in the *Double Eagle II*, landing in France some 137 hours later.

First Solo Atlantic Crossing in a Helium Balloon

Air Force Col. Joe Kittinger became the first person to solo across the Atlantic in a helium balloon, leaving from a field in Caribou on September 14, 1984. Kittinger made the trip in the *Rosie O'Grady*, covering 3,543 miles in eighty-six hours eventually landing in Italy.

First Transatlantic Hot Air Balloon Crossing

Sir Richard Branson and Per Lindstrand lifted off from Sugarloaf on July 2, 1987, in the *Virgin Atlantic Flyer*. Aided by the Jet Stream, they floated 3,075 miles to the United Kingdom, landing on July 3, after nearly thirty-two hours aloft, at times traveling at 130 miles per hour.

Heaviest Female Marathoner

Ragen Chastain of Los Angeles, California, set the record for the heaviest female marathoner on Earth at Sanford on May 14, 2017, during the Mainly Marathons race. The 288-pound runner finished dead last with a time of ten hours, three minutes.

World's Longest Canoe

A canoe measuring 149 feet was built by students and teachers of Nokomis Regional High School in Newport in 2006. It was unveiled and launched on Sebasticook Lake on July 8.

Largest Collection of Umbrella Covers

Nancy Hoffman of Peaks Island has converted part of her home into an Umbrella Cover Museum. Her collection includes 730 different covers.

Eartha, the largest revolving globe, is located at the DeLorme Building in Yarmouth.
Courtesy of Garmin.

Largest Revolving Globe

It took two years to construct and finish the world's largest rotating globe, Eartha, located in an atrium at Garmin, a mapping and GPS software firm in Yarmouth. It is 41 feet in diameter.

Longest Lobster Roll

The world record for longest lobster roll was set in Portland in June 2009 at 61 feet, 9.5 inches on Commercial Street. It took forty-five pounds of picked lobster meat and four gallons of Miracle Whip. The roll was baked at Amato's. Linda Bean's Maine Lobster donated the meat. The stunt raised $3,600 for a local charity. That record was later eclipsed in July 2017 by a 181-foot lobster roll in Shediac, New Brunswick.

Fastest Mile in Swim Fins

Brunswick High School Student Zachary Miller holds the record for running a mile in swim fins in the fastest time. In July 2014, it took him five minutes and 48.86 seconds.

Most Pine Boards Broken With One Hand

Karate instructor Donna Harris in Lewiston broke an astounding 156 pine boards with her bare hands in less than a minute in Lewiston in October 2015.

Fastest Completion of a Game of Myst

Dylan Guptill of South Berwick took just three minutes and eighteen seconds to finish this video adventure on August 22, 2007.

Fastest Bicycle Trip Along East Coast

Brendan Walsh of Ashburnham, Massachusetts, set out from Madawaska on September 30, 2019, and bicycled to Key West, Florida, in a time of 11 days, 9 hours, and 32 minutes, setting an unofficial record. He is waiting to hear from the Guinness folks for final certification.

World's Longest Cat

Barivel, the most el grande domestic gato in the world, lives in Italy, but is a Maine Coon Cat. From nose to end of tail he measures three-feet, eleven-inches long.

Addendum

Although the *Guinness Book* doesn't have such a category, what is believed to be the World's Largest Ice Carousel was made in January 2019 on Long Lake in Sinclair. It measured 427 feet across and was up to three feet thick. Outboard motors provided locomotion.

Down
East

Down East

For many the label "Down East," seems synonymous with all of coastal Maine, but in reality this nautical term is most appropriately applied to a single geographical area. It is bounded on the west by the mighty Penobscot River, on the north by Interstate 95, on the east by the border with New Brunswick and on the south by the sea.

Few people, however, know why to go "Down" East you must go "up" the coast.

The most satisfactory explanation is that "Down East" is a seafaring term born because the prevailing wind blows from the southwest. Schooners and clipper ships going to Maine from the west and south sailed before the wind, a practice described as "running downhill" because of the smooth sailing when compared to "beating up against it," going to windward.

Vessels running before the wind were said to be "running their easting down." Thus, a sailing vessel bound to Maine would "run" before the wind and go "downhill to the eastward," or, if you will, go "Down East."

Interesting things to see, do, and discover Down East begin for many when they cross the Penobscot River on the magnificent cable-stay suspension bridge which features an observatory atop the western tower. Nearby in Bucksport is the famous roadside cemetery with its "cursed" gravestone—and it only gets better from there.

From the geological and natural wonders of Acadia National Park to the 45th Parallel Monument in Perry marking the exact halfway point from the North Pole to the Equator, from Lead Mountain along the historic "Airline" north of Beddington, where Confederate President Jefferson Davis literally slept, to the tale of a body buried in a rum barrel in Cutler on the coast, to Lubec which is home to the nation's easternmost point, and a terrifying whirlpool or two, there's much to discover here.

Previous page, clockwise from the top, the magnificent Penobscot Narrows Bridge and Observatory (Courtesy Maine Department of Transportation), Bar Harbor's "Magic Ship," the Kronprinzessin Cecilie (From Author's Collection), the missing French aircraft the White Bird, (Courtesy Digicommons) and Shopworn guide Molunkus Harry was a popular postcard theme during the 1960s. (From Author's Collection).

School Has Snack That Will Not Die

Rumor has it that one of America's favorite snack cakes, the Hostess Twinkie, is the perfect survival food for people looking to outlast the apocalypse. And at a high school in Blue Hill, science students have been conducting an experiment to prove that the idea might not be so far-fetched.

Since 1976 an unwrapped Twinkie has remained intact inside a glass case at George Stevens Academy. While looking a little paler than the day it was made, it remains flexible and mold-free despite the passing of more than four decades.

Twinkies have been around since 1930. Over the years an urban myth took root that because the Twinkie has so many preservatives they can last forever. The company, however, officially states that the optimum shelf life is just twenty-five days.

Teacher Roger Bennatti decided a Twinkie experiment was the perfect way to educate his chemistry class about food additives and shelf life. When students brought a package to class, he ate one and placed the other one on a blackboard. It was later moved to a case.

The irony is that the school's Twinkie, now on display for forty-four years, outlasted Interstate Bakeries, the company that made it, but which filed for bankruptcy in 2012. And outlasted Bennatti, who has long since retired.

The Twinkie case now resides in the office of Assistant Head of the School Libby Rosemeier, who was a student in Bennatti's chemistry class in 1976. *Maine Atlas: M15, B4*

Pound Protected Fields and Livestock

In a colonial community the last thing anyone would tolerate was livestock running loose, getting into gardens, or damaging crops. So, one of the first public works projects undertaken by early settlers of Orrington was to create a sturdy stockade where wayward animals were kept until claimed by their owner.

Orrington was incorporated in 1788, three years before Bangor, although robust settlement didn't begin until the early 1800s when the Town Pound was built. A wooden stockade, erected in 1807, was later replaced with the current, thirty-five-foot-diameter circular stone structure with a single iron gate in 1843. Unlike other towns that used loose stone, Orrington's Pound, located on Route 15 just north of the Penobscot Energy Recovery Plant, was laid up with mortar.

Each year the town's "Pound Keeper," was required to provide detailed records of all related transactions including fines for loose animals that damaged crops and ended up in the pound, and advertising to find the owners of lost animals.

At different times in its history, Orrington has been in Hancock, Lincoln, and Penobscot counties as those boundaries shifted. *Maine Atlas: M23, C2*

Scientist Finds His 'Groove' Near Ellsworth

The basic tenets of science have always encountered resistance from those who would rather believe in myth. That was certainly the case when it came to deciphering the geology of New England in the mid-1800s. A "Great Deluge," perhaps even the flood of Noah, was thought responsible for features we understand as connected to glaciation today. Some even believe glacial erratic boulders found atop mountains, were placed there by giants.

While on a trip to Maine in 1864, Harvard scientist Louis Agassiz identified deep grooves and surface polish in an outcrop of bedrock in Ellsworth Falls that helped him develop the continental glaciation theory that is the gold standard today.

The nomination papers for the National Register of Historic Places notes that the ledges symbolize "a major landmark in natural science, geological thinking and is a monument to modern scientific thought."

Agassiz went on to help found the Smithsonian and the National

Academy of Sciences. His "ledge" can be found next to the parking lot of a business on the west side of US Route 1A just north of downtown. *Maine Atlas: M24, E1*

Amulet's Origins Shrouded in Mystery

Grand Lake Stream Amulet.
Courtesy of Digicommons.

From time to time, Maine has been home to discoveries that raise new questions about the earliest people to live on this continent and those who may have visited long before the age of European exploration.

One such enigma surfaced in 1990 near Grand Lake Stream, where there are well-documented rock petroglyphs.

Walter Elliot, who first reported the petroglyphs in 1988, discovered a small, slate-covered tomb or void in the ground containing multiple stone artifacts with symbols and images on them. Among them was a small, amulet-like stone and another stone that was slender, but nearly thirteen inches long. Elliot was an amateur archeologist who believed there was evidence of Viking settlements in Eastern Maine.

Maine archeologists who have looked at what has become known as the Grand Lake Stream Amulet and the other items have yet to determine their origin or authenticity. They do not appear to be characteristic of Native American creations. "Although the site is undoubtedly human-made, its function, antiquity, and cultural attribution cannot be precisely specified on the basis of the unique characteristics of both the artifacts and the cist[void]," a preliminary report says. That's a lot of words to basically say, "Beats me."

The petroglyphs are on the National Register of Historic Places. The exact location is not widely disseminated to protect it from vandalism.

Maine Atlas: M35, B4

Tidal Falls Offer Twice the Fun

Popular with kayakers who can enjoy the rapids and waves on both incoming and outgoing tides at the entrance/exit to Salt Pond, Reversing Falls on state Route 175 in Blue Hill is one of several such phenomena in New England.

Conditions are optimal about two and a half hours before a high tide when a standing wave nearly three feet high can form. Because of the ever-present rocks and cold water temperatures, only experienced boaters with proper equipment should attempt to run this narrow channel.

Part of what makes the spot so attractive is a graceful, concrete "rainbow" arch span over the waterway. Falls Bridge, built in 1926, will not be there forever. It is slated for replacement in 2022. The new bridge will be wider and make accommodation for pedestrians, while associated work will improve access to the falls.

Another, smaller reversing falls can be found nearby where Route 175 crosses the tidal Bagaduce River in Brooksville. *Maine Atlas: M15, B5*

Witch's Curse is Compelling Tale

Perhaps the most famous "haunted monument" in Maine, the witch's foot on Col. Jonathan Buck's monument in Bucksport, the town he founded on the banks of the Penobscot River, has aroused curiosity for decades.

Legend holds that Buck ordered a witch put to death by burning at the stake and that during that horrible deed her leg rolled out of the conflagration. After the impressive granite obelisk was erected over his tomb, a stain in the shape of a leg and foot appeared in the stone. Generations of descendants reportedly tried scrubbing the stain off, and even replacing the stone, to no avail, resulting in the belief that Buck's grave is cursed.

That's a great story, but no witches were ever tried, much less put to death in Maine. And, the stain actually is on a monument erected in Buck's honor nearly one hundred years after his death. His modest tombstone elsewhere in the well-marked cemetery on Route 1, across from the town's grocery store, is unblemished.

Buck was a justice of the peace, built the town's first sawmill, general store and first boat in the area. He died in 1795 at age 60. *Maine Atlas: M23, E2*

Champlain Cross has Contemporary Origins

Hikers on the North Ridge Trail on Acadia National Park's Cadillac Mountain have often wondered about a cross chiseled in the pink granite bedrock. For years, people believed it was left there by the crew of French explorer Samuel de Champlain, who charted the area in 1604 and named it "L'Isle des Monts-deserts," or literally Island of Barren Mountains.

The story fails to take into account how much time it would have taken those sailors to repeatedly bushwhack to that spot over the several days necessary to carve the cross into such dense stone.

Subsequent investigation in the twentieth century showed that there are actually four crosses and associated iron pins, and that they correspond exactly with the corners of a lot of land sold to the Hancock County Trustees for Public Reservations in 1908. The Trustees' holdings eventually became Sieur de Monts National Monument in 1916 which was later renamed to Lafayette National Park in 1919. The name was changed to Acadia in 1929.

Survey sleuths believe that the crosses were created when the property lines were established in 1880s. *Maine Atlas: M16, B4*

Homage to Unknown Baby

Graves of unknown river drivers are fairly common in Maine, but along the St. Croix River, which forms part of the boundary with New Brunswick, there is a grave that tugs at even the hardest heartstrings.

Called the "Unknown Baby's Grave," a simple stone, surrounded by a small iron-pipe enclosure, memorializes a tragedy that unfolded in 1899.

A group of burly river drivers discovered the body of a tiny baby, sewn into a pillowcase, while trying to clear a jam near a place called Duck Point.

The men walked across the jam to the American side and, with what little ceremony they could muster, buried the infant. They speculated it had been thrown from a train crossing the river in Vanceboro, eight miles upstream.

A year later, a marker was erected, and successive generations of river runners have taken care of it. It is located directly behind the campsite of the same name.

The St. Croix is an unusual trip in that the left of the river is Canada, and the right is the United States. There's an hour time difference from one side to the other. And, when it's zero degrees (Celsius) in Canada, it's a comparatively balmy-sounding 32 degrees Fahrenheit in Maine. Access to the site is only possible by kayak or canoe. *Maine Atlas: M46, D3*

Venerable Garage Recalls Author's Legacy

Among the many iconic locations featured in Robert McCloskey's four books set in Maine is Condon's Garage in Bucks Harbor.

His book *One Morning in Maine* provides a timeless look at the lives of a family exploring Maine using the author's wife and daughters as models. The McCloskeys had a summer place on Scott Island off Little Deer Isle.

The book won the Caldecott Honor in 1953. The area also inspired McCloskey to write *Blueberries for Sal*.

Built in 1925 by Ralph Condon, the building on Route 176 was originally slated to include not just the garage, but a store, and maybe even a movie house upstairs. Those other operations never happened and Condon's sons, Russ and John Richard (whom everyone called Dick) ran the place until World War II when it shut down so they could work in shipyards. After the war Russ opened a store down the street and Dick reopened the garage.

Other family members ran the business until July 2007 when the auto repair operation moved and the building was put up for sale. *Maine Atlas: M15, B3*

Night of the Nazi Spies

World War II touched Maine in several ways, but none as dramatic as the night a German submarine, *U-1230*, put two Nazi spies ashore in the sleepy village of Hancock as part of a caper dubbed "Operation Magpie."

William Colepaugh and Erick Gimpel were ferried ashore in a rubber raft on Nov. 29, 1944. They made their way to a nearby road carrying suitcases containing clothes, $60,000 in American cash, the makings of a radio, and a handful of diamonds.

Nazi spies who landed under cover of darkness in Hancock during World War II were eventually arrested in New York City. *Courtesy of Wikicommons.*

Fortunately, they were spotted walking along a road in a light snow squall by 17-year-old Harvard Hodgkins. The enterprising lad followed their tracks and noticed they came abruptly out of the woods. He found the raft and then told his father, who called the local sheriff.

The spies, sent to learn about America's atomic bomb program, were tracked by the FBI to New York City and eventually captured and sentenced to death. Their death sentences were commuted and they were eventually released.

Meanwhile, Hodgkins was given a tour of New York and got to meet boxer Joe Lewis and Babe Ruth. He passed away in 1984.

However, it was not all good news. While leaving the Gulf of Maine on Dec. 3, 1944, *U-1230* torpedoed a Canadian freighter carrying molasses, resulting in forty-two deaths. *Maine Atlas: M16, A4*

Graceful Bridge Sets State Records

With towers standing taller than the Statue of Liberty, the Penobscot Narrows Bridge over the Penobscot River between Prospect and Verona Island is considered the most spectacular span in Maine. The multi-level observatory deck in the west tower, some 428 feet above the water, is the highest such structure in the world, according to the Maine Department of Transportation. The elevator to access the

Weird!

'Big Jim' Witness to Titanic Changes

Standing tall over the former Stinson Sardine Canning plant on Route 186 in Prospect Harbor, "Big Jim" has been an iconic figure along the coast of Maine.

The plant, built in 1906, was the last remaining sardine packer in the country. It was shut down by Bumblebee Brands in 2010. That closure ended a 134-year tradition of sardine canning at fifty-six plants in Maine. At its peak, the industry produced more than 300 million cans of sardines a year.

Over the years, Big Jim has held giant tins of

observatory is the tallest in Maine.

The span is 2,120 feet and the deck which carries US Route 1 and State Route 3, is a full 135 feet above the river, allowing for the passage of large ships. The bridge cost $85 million to build. The center section, at some 1,161 feet long, is the longest single span in Maine.

Opened in December 2006, the concrete, cable-stay suspension bridge replaced a smaller steel suspension bridge built in 1931 for just over $850,000. Multiple epoxy-coated steel cables on the new bridge are enclosed in a protective plastic sheath. Each sheath is filled with nitrogen gas to inhibit corrosion.

Nearby is historic Fort Knox, a large granite structure completed in 1869, to guard the Penobscot River. Its sixty-four cannons never fired a shot in conflict. *Maine Atlas: M23, E2*

Line in the Sand Defines Nation

Archimedes famously said "Give me a place to stand and I'll move the world." A no less Herculean task awaited the US Coast Survey in 1857 when it was directed by Congress to create super accurate maps of the nation. The question was: where to start?

Beach Cliff Sardines, and currently clutches a wood lobster trap. When first created in the 1950s, Big Jim, was located along the Maine Turnpike in Kittery where it welcomed tourists to both "Vacationland," and "Sardineland." Destined for the dump, the sign was rescued by Charles Stinson and moved to his cannery in the early 1980s.

Originally two-sided and made of wood, the flat, thirty-foot tall sign was rebuilt out of aluminum after Big Jim lost his pants in a windstorm.

Since the plant closed, the facility—which includes the plant and deep-water wharf—has been used by several struggling seafood operations including a lobster processor and dealer.

Nearby, Prospect Harbor Lighthouse has guided mariners for centuries. It was commissioned by President George Washington.

Maine Atlas: M17, B1

A vintage postcard image of "Big Jim." *From Author's Collection.*

Surveyors decided to create a series of ten super-straight baselines from Maine to Georgia and then triangulate from there.

In Maine, a site in the blueberry barrens on the Epping Plain, north of Harrington, was chosen. Crews measured, remeasured and then measured again before establishing monuments at each end. A rough road, now called the Baseline Road, was built across the sandy plain.

The work was overseen by Benjamin Franklin's great-grandson Alexander Bache and inspected by none other than Jefferson Davis, who later became president of the Confederate States of America.

Although the actual marble monuments were moved to the Maine State Museum in Augusta and the Cherryfield Historical Society, the granite bases remain. The Epping Baseline is the only one of the ten that can still be visited. The eastern end base is next to a dirt road on blueberry company land. Please respect private property and do not pick berries or damage plants. *Maine Atlas: M25, C3*

Ghostly Tale Adapts Over Time

Like any good Maine ghost story, the legend of the spirit of Catherine's Hill along Route 182 in Franklin has something for everyone. Also known as the Black Woods Road, Route 182 reportedly is haunted by the ghost of a woman named Catherine who, depending on whom you believe, died horribly not far from Fox Pond in either the 1860s, 1930s, or 1970s. The ghost purportedly wanders the woods and hills and approaches wary travelers in the dead of night looking for her head, which she lost in a carriage or auto accident. Other accounts claim the ghost flags down motorists on foggy nights and asks for rides to Bar Harbor. Those who do not stop, the legend holds, "will suffer the consequences."

Nearby 962-foot-tall Catherine Mountain is reportedly named for one of the area's early settlers and that name was recorded long before automobiles were invented.

The area is the heart of the state's Donnell Pond Public Reserve Land, which includes beautiful hiking trails, sandy lakeside camping spots, and several summits featuring incredible views. Ghost or not, it's worth a visit for that alone. *Maine Atlas: M24, D5*

Galamander was a Heavy Hauler

Sounding more like some kind of reptile than a piece of stone-cutting history, the Robertson Quarry Galamander in Franklin is the only one of its design left.

Stretching nearly eighteen feet long, the galamander was a large wooden-wheeled wagon designed specifically for lifting and moving large pieces of granite out of a quarry. It consisted of a heavy-duty wood frame, rudimentary seat, and stout brakes. Horses or oxen provided the power. The stone was carried under, not on top of, the frame.

Galamanders were used in quarries throughout the state in the late 1800s and early 1900s. Franklin had more than fifteen quarries in its history. The Robertson Quarry Galamander was rescued from an abandoned pit in Franklin in 1965 and placed under a protective roof along State Route 182 at the junction with Grist Mill Road. It is on the National Register of Historic Places.

Credit for the overall design is given to the Rev. W.H. Littlefield on the island of Vinalhaven, and a replica of a galamander is on display. *Maine Atlas: M24, D4*

Cutler's Forlorn Casket of Rum

When the three-masted brig *Lena Thurlow* hove into the bay off Cutler in the late summer of 1873, watchers on shore could not help but notice her pennant at half-staff, indicating there had been a death on board.

Once at the dock, Capt. Tristam Thurlow Corbett, himself just 27 -years-old, announced that his blushing bride, Jeanette, 26, had died

Sea captain's wife Jeanette Corbett, age 26, of Cutler died of a tropical disease in Cuba in 1873 and was brought back to Maine in a barrel of rum.
From Author's Collection.

of some unknown tropical disease weeks earlier while the vessel was loading a cargo of rum, sugar, and other items in Matanzas, Cuba. Among those trying to absorb the horrible news were Jeanette's parents, Capt. Sam Blunt and his wife, Ann.

On her deathbed, Jeanette asked her beloved to bring her back and bury her in Maine. Without any means of refrigeration, however, some ingenuity was required. Capt. Corbett secured a large wooden barrel at the rum distillery in Cuba, placed Jeanette inside, and filled it with the potent local spirit. She spent the ride back in the hold with the other cargo.

Yellow fever was rampant in Cuba at the time, so not knowing what malady may have killed her, the good people of Cutler were reticent to open the cask to prepare her for burial. Ultimately it was decided to dig a deep, circular hole, and inter her in the barrel. Her gravestone today is in the Old Cutler Cemetery at the corner of Little Machias and Cutler roads in Cutler. *Maine Atlas: M27, D1*

Future Confederate President Visits Maine Mountain

Three years before he became the president of the Confederate States, Jefferson Davis spent time in the hills and barrens of Down East Maine. Davis, a US senator and former US secretary of war, visited US Coast Survey crews on the blueberry barrens in Epping in 1858.

He and his wife, Varina, stopped at Lead Mountain, which was then called Humpback Mountain, in Beddington. They spent three weeks in tents atop the mountain in the survey crew's camp, which was run by an old friend, Alexander Dallas Bache, Benjamin Franklin's great-grandson. A trail to the summit was later called the Jeff Davis Road.

Legend holds that at one point during his visit, Davis left a mysterious trunk at the Schoppee House Inn in Beddington with instructions that only someone with a password could claim it—which someone did several months later. Some have speculated (wildly) that it contained plans for the Civil War, but more likely it held surveying documents.

Also that year, Davis made a stop in Portland and gave a speech about the importance of national unity at a home at the corner of Park and Danforth streets. He also visited the Henry Knox Mansion in Thomaston. *Maine Atlas: M24, A5*

'Magic Ship' Held Lure of Gold

Residents of Bar Harbor were amazed to wake up on the morning of August 14, 1916, to find a gigantic ocean liner anchored in Frenchman Bay. The German ship *Kronprinzessin Cecilie* was nearly all the way to England when she turned around to avoid being seized by the British or French when its captain learned of the outbreak of World War I. Capt. Charles Polack had the vessel's funnels painted with black tops to appear to be a British vessel. Passengers were not happy about the change of plans. Two American millionaires on board reportedly asked to buy the ship so she could be reflagged as American.

Along with 1,216 passengers and 700 crew, the 706-foot-long "Magic Ship," as she would later be called, was also loaded with riches: Some $10.68 million in gold and $3 million in silver were on board.

After several days, US Navy ships arrived, and the passengers and crew were allowed to disembark and take trains to New York. The precious metal was seized by US Marshals. The vessel was later commandeered by the Navy and became the troop transport USS *Mount Vernon*. It was scrapped in 1940. *Maine Atlas: M16, B4*

A Place Just Wild about Blueberries

You may be crazy about blueberries, but you haven't seen it all until you've visited Wild Blueberry Land on US Route 1 in Columbia Falls. The entire seven-acre property is an homage to Maine's Official Fruit.

Created to help smaller blueberry farmers in the area, Wild Blueberry Land features a dome retail store that is billed as the World's Largest Blueberry. Outside, old nautical buoys have been repurposed as giant berries and a satellite dish is now a blueberry pie. Old winnowing machines are on display in the parking area.

Along with buying all manner of blueberry items, memorabilia, and food products such as jams, jellies, pastries, spreads, candy, ice cream and maple syrup, you can also take a photo with the Blueberry Throne or play miniature golf.

The popular attraction was once featured in a segment of the comic strip "Zippy."

Wild Blueberry Land is open seasonally, when, of course, there are plenty of fresh blueberries from area fields for sale. *Maine Atlas: M25, D5*

Marker is Hemisphere's Halfway Point

Plenty of places in Maine and the country claim to be on the 45th parallel, the line that is exactly halfway between the North Pole and the Equator.

But the granite marker along US Route 1 in Perry is the real deal, in addition to being the first place in North America so marked. Crews working for the US Coast and Geodesic Survey placed a brass pin along the road in 1896. Like Alexander Bache who laid out the Epping Baseline, the crew's leader Charles Meigs Bache, was a great-grandson of Benjamin Franklin. Among the others on the crew was Alexander Wadsworth Longfellow, brother of the famous poet.

The good people of Perry ordered a special engraved block of granite to mark the spot in 1899. It can be found in a small park and picnic area on the side of the road.

Modern surveying techniques have revealed that the actual 45th parallel is about 140 feet north of the marker perhaps helping inspire the old Maine expression "close enough for government work." *Maine Atlas: M37, E2*

'Leatherface' was Beloved Maine Neighbor

Few people know that Mount Desert Island was the longtime home of one of the movie industry's scariest cannibals, the bloody butcher, Leatherface from *The Texas Chainsaw Massacre*.

Actor Gunnar Hansen lived quietly next to the library in Northeast Harbor where he was active in the community. Many friends and neighbors did not know he once appeared on film as a leather apron-wearing villain that drapes his victims' skins over his face and dismembered people with a chain saw.

In 1974, the Icelandic-born Hansen was living in Austin, Texas, when he auditioned for the part of Leatherface in the low-budget film.

Roles in *Demon Lover* and the spoof *Hollywood Chainsaw Hookers*, quickly followed, earning Hansen a cult following.

Back in Maine, the hulking but soft-spoken Hansen was an accomplished and erudite magazine and script writer and editor. He worked on local histories, a travel memoir, and the book *Chain Saw Confidential*, a behind-the-scenes look at the making of the original film.

He died at home in 2015. *Maine Atlas: M16, C3*

Lobster Trap Trees Celebrate Christmas

In the most heavily forested state in the nation (90 percent tree coverage) Maine has no shortage of Christmas trees. However, in an effort to impart some semblance of individuality, and celebrate local culture, several communities have embraced unique options for public representations of the holiday's iconic symbol.

In "The County," Fort Fairfield celebrates with a town Christmas Tree constructed entirely of potato barrels. In Trenton the Trenton Bridge Lobster Pound adds wreaths and garlands to a twenty-foot-tall pyramid of wooden lobster "cars," wooden crates used by fishermen to store their live catch on moorings.

At thirty-nine feet high, the largest in the world, Maine's Colossus of Christmas is the stately Lobster Trap Tree in Mildred Merrill Park on Main Street in Rockland where the annual Seafood Festival is held in summer. Each winter citizen volunteers use plastic cable ties to join more than 150 wire lobster traps together and decorate it as a Christmas tree. Decorations include 2,500 lights and 100 lobster buoy ornaments. Since 2005, the entire community gathers for the official lighting of the tree just after Thanksgiving during the Festival of Lights.

Maine communities with similar installations include Kennebunkport, York, Stonington, Jonesport and Lubec. *Maine Atlas: M79, B2*

Lubec's Amazing Phantom Gold Rush

The frontiers and edges of America have always had their share of con artists and hustlers. Lubec, Maine, in 1898 was no exception.

It seems ludicrous today that anyone would fall for a scheme where an entrepreneur convinces people that he has developed a process whereby solid gold can be extracted from simple sea water.

Smooth-talking Baptist minister Prescott Jernegan founded the Electrolytic Marine Salts Company claiming that when his "accumulators" (actually large cast-iron pots) were lowered into the ocean and electricity was turned on, they would harvest millions of dollars in gold. He claimed each cubic mile of sea water contained as much as $100 million in gold.

Investors from New York, Massachusetts, and Connecticut were shown multiple pieces of gold and nuggets when the accumulators were retrieved each morning. The fact was, it was the same handful of gold deposited during the dark of night by his partner Charles Fisher who was a skilled diver.

Like any Ponzi scheme, it fell apart once the money from new rubes dried up and there wasn't any cash to pay out to earlier investors. Within a year, Jernegan and Fisher, along with hundreds of thousands of dollars, vanished, the former fleeing to Europe. No charges were ever filed. *Maine Atlas: M27, A3*

Navy Born from Machias Resistance

Referred to by James Fenimore Cooper as "The Lexington of the Seas," the town of Machias engaged the British in the first naval battle of the Revolution in early June of 1775.

The good townspeople gathered around copious mugs of rum at the Burnham Tavern, voted to refuse to do business with a loyalist merchant seeking to sell his goods in return for lumber for the British Army in Boston. The merchant's vessels *Polly* and *Unity* had been accompanied by the HMS *Margaretta*.

Led by Col. Benjamin Foster, militia men from up and down the coast, armed with little more than pitchforks and hunting rifles, seized the *Unity* and commandeered a local schooner, the *Falmouth Packet*. Capt. Jeremiah O'Brien and a crew of area patriots, sailing in the larger and faster *Unity*, caught up with the *Margaretta* and attacked. The crew of the *Packet* joined the fray and the *Margaretta* was taken. Two Machias men were killed. Four British sailors, including Capt. James Moore perished.

Captains O'Brien and Foster went on to capture additional British vessels during the war and helped repel an attack on Machias by one thousand British troops in 1777.

Cannons and other arms from the *Margaretta* helped protect Machias Bay for the duration of the conflict. *Maine Atlas: M26, C4*

Shopworn guide Molunkus Harry was a popular postcard theme during 1960s. *From Author's Collection.*

Colorful Character Promoted Sporting Life

Pictured smoking a pipe, wearing rumpled clothes, badly in need of a shave, and with somewhat bloodshot eyes, the mythical Maine Guide Molunkus Harry was a popular postcard subject during the 1960s when the image was used to attract "sports" to a hunting and fishing sporting camp on remote Molunkus Lake east of Medway.

The image was based on a painting by Wesley Herrick, proprietor of Harry's Fishing and Hunting Lodge on Molunkus

Lake. Several of Herrick's whimsical hunting paintings were turned into postcards by Eastern Illustrating Company of Belfast. Herrick, a guide who founded Camp Wanderlust for Boys on Chesuncook Lake in the 1930s, has been described as "The Mark Twain of the Allagash."

The word Molunkus means "stream in a ravine," but based on the character of Harry, it has also come to be associated with galoot, oaf, or klutz.

The exploits of Harry have been profiled in a book called "Short Stories from the Maine Woods," by Steve Nissley. If you don't have six bucks for the book, the website says the author will trade you for his favorite brand of gunpowder, bullets, or permission to hunt on your land. *Maine Atlas: M44, A3*

Largest Loon Overlooks Lakes

A relative newcomer in the pantheon of oversized outdoor deities in Maine, the giant loon that overlooks the waterfront in downtown Lincoln was unveiled in October of 2016. To some it stands, or sits actually, as a symbol of the recreational draw of the town's more than a dozen lakes. During the annual Loon Festival each July it gets decorated with giant necklaces and other accessories.

The thirteen-foot-long by six-foot-tall fiberglass installation was built by the Fiberglas Farm of Belfast for the cost of $13,000 which, some residents argued, was just "looney." However, it instantly became a favorite selfie spot and has served its intended purpose, which was to promote the region to vacationers and encourage them to linger a little longer in the downtown of a community still recovering from the closure of its economic mainstay, a pulp and paper mill.

While no one has yet claimed it's the largest of its kind in the US or the world, there's no doubt it is the grandest of its kind in Maine.

Lincoln's Loon is located in a small park with a gazebo at the intersection of Route 2 and Main Street on the shore of Mattanawcook Pond. *Maine Atlas: M43, E5*

Living The Good Life Was Couple's Calling

Literally writing the book on *Living the Good Life*, Scott and Helen Nearing moved to Harborside in 1952 to "liberate ourselves from the cruder forms of exploitation; the plunder of the planet, the slavery of man and beast, the slaughter of men in war, and animals for food."

From that self-built stone house called Forest Farm, the couple became thought leaders of the back-to-the-land movement and the trend toward living more simply. The Nearings, who were inducted into the Vegetarian Hall of Fame in 1991, tended their own organic garden and grew and preserved all their own food. Between them they wrote and published more than fifty books.

Scott Nearing died at age 100 in 1983. Helen died in an automobile crash, at age 91, in 1995.

The Good Life Center, located off the Harborside Road, is a nonprofit educational and retreat organization established on the Nearing homestead after their deaths to preserve their legacy. Along with preserving the house, gardens and properties, the center holds public events, operates an online bookstore, and offers tours and conducts a residency program. *Maine Atlas: M15, C2*

Pioneering Spirit Watches Over River

Paddlers running the Machias River will discover an unusual memorial should they pause at an island just downstream from the unrunnable Holmes Falls.

In the middle of the small, tree-covered Deadman's Island, located between the upper and lower section of the falls, is the grave of Obadiah Hill, one of the first settlers of Machias, who went on to be a successful merchant and lumberman.

Hill, reportedly died in a drowning in an accident while running logs through Holmes Falls on May 28, 1786. He was 34 years old.

Without access to a proper coffin, his compatriots reportedly placed the body in a pork barrel and hastily buried it on the island. In 1905, his grandchildren erected a proper gravestone noting Hill was "A pioneer of Old Machias."

Hill helped build the first meeting house in the area in 1774. He also was aboard the schooner *Unity* when it attacked and captured the British vessel HMS *Margaretta* in the first naval battle of the American Revolution in 1775.

The island is accessible by canoe or kayak although it is possible to wade to it from the northern shore during periods of low water. *Maine Atlas: M25, B5*

Road Flies High with Tales of Wolves

There are many legendary stretches of road in Maine, but perhaps none so famous as "The Airline," an east-west track stretching from Brewer to Calais and named for the intrepid stagecoach company that once traveled its rugged track.

Now known as State Route 9, the Airline was originally laid out in the early 1800s as a way to attract settlers to the area. At first it was called "General Cobb's Great Road from the Penobscot to the Schoodic [St. Croix River]," and was barely passable by oxcart. Later it was called Black's Road after John Black, a landowner's agent who went on to find prominence in Ellsworth where he built a mansion. By the mid-1800s, stagecoaches were using the road although fanciful engravings of the era showed them beset by wolves and bandits.

Parts of the Airline weren't plowed in winter until the 1930s. Hills then were once so steep that Model-T cars had to ascend in reverse. Since 1970, the road has been vastly improved and serves as a high-speed connector between Interstate 95 and New Brunswick.

One unique feature, a 2.5-mile-long glacial esker in Aurora called the Whalesback, now features a viewpoint and rest stop. Geologist Louis Agassiz identified it in 1860 and noted it was as much as 320 feet high. *Maine Atlas: M24, A3*

Monument to Missing Colonists Disappears

Why did a monument to colonists who vanished after a shipwreck on Mount Desert suddenly disappear? It is because the story and the tragedy it commemorated was all a lie.

Ship Harbor, in Acadia National Park, looks to be the perfect place for an eighteenth century maritime disaster. Legend held the colonists on the vessel *Grand Design* mistook the mouth of a cove for a river in 1741. The vessel wrecked on an offshore ledge and a handful of survivors endured a harsh winter. Later, those who attempted to walk through the wilderness for help, were never heard from again.

Apparently ill-informed scribes in 1853 in the town of Warren crafted the legend out of the true story of the *Martha and Eliza*, a ship that wrecked on Grand Manan Island, in the Bay of Fundy. The *Grand Design* was the name of the ship's mission to bring colonists to Pennsylvania. If not for the generosity and help of the Passamaquoddy Indians, many of the shipwrecked colonists would have died.

The false narrative was so strong that a tablet noting the disaster was put up at Ship Harbor by well-meaning citizens in the early 1900s. The National Park Service later removed the monument. *Maine Atlas: M16, D3*

Museum Talks the Talk on Telephony

Along with rural electrification, perhaps no twentieth century technology transformed rural living in Maine more than the hard-wired telephone. The history of that utility is preserved and celebrated in the New England Museum of Telephony on the Winkumpaugh Road in Ellsworth.

Starting with Alexander Graham Bell's invention in 1876, the museum's exhibits follow developments including switchboards, rotary dial phones, and gear from switching offices and substations. While Bell gets all the credit, it was equipment invented by Kansas City undertaker Almon Strowger in 1891 that really allowed telephony to catch fire.

On the grounds can be found the original small wood structure that housed the former telephone company—the country's smallest—in the island village of Frenchboro.

A large archive of photographs, tools, and working plug and wire switchboards can be seen along with more than five hundred phones including a pink "Princess" rotary phone and a red desktop model actually used by NASA to communicate with the US Navy during spacecraft recoveries.

It's open Saturday afternoons in July, August, and September. Of course, to be safe, you can always call ahead. *Maine Atlas: M23, D5*

'Bert and I' had Ties to Arctic's Byrd

Maine can lay claim to ties to two intrepid polar explorers, both Admiral Robert Peary and Admiral Richard Byrd who savored time at his historic log lodge "Wickyup," on the shores of Tunk Lake in Hancock County. It was there where Byrd planned three of his expeditions to the Antarctic.

Previously, on May 9, 1926, he and copilot Floyd Bennett became the first to fly over the North Pole. He was also first to fly over the South Pole on November 29, 1929.

A former wilderness clubhouse for wealthy summer residents, the 12,000-square-foot, two-story Wickyup was purchased by Byrd in the late 1930s. He reportedly wrote his book *Alone: The Classic Polar Adventure*, while drifting around Tunk Lake in a rowboat. Byrd died in 1957.

Few know, however, of Wickyup's ties to the late Robert Bryan, who partnered with the late Marshall Dodge to produce the series of

Admiral Richard Byrd, who flew this aircraft over the North Pole, maintained a log lodge on Tunk Lake in Down East Maine.
Courtesy of Digicommons.

"Bert and I" comedy records that introduced the nation to Maine's understated style of Down East humor. The lodge was built by Bryan's grandfather and the family continued to own an adjacent camp for years after Byrd moved in.

Wickyup, which was put on the National Register of Historic Places in 1970, was destroyed in a fire set by an arsonist in 1984. *Maine Atlas: M25, E1*

Norse Coin Suggests Ties to Vikings

Columbus' claim to being the first European to reach the new world suffered a major hit when archeologists in 1960 confirmed a Viking settlement in Newfoundland dating to 1,000 AD. Legends hold, however, that the Norsemen ranged even farther afield, reaching south all the way to Martha's Vineyard and even west into Minnesota.

Maine has no shortage of reported evidence that Vikings visited the area, ranging from the Spirit Pond Runestones found in Phippsburg in 1971, to Norse Pond in Cutler, and items excavated near Grand Lake Stream.

Now known as "The Maine Penny," a Norse coin dating to 1,100 AD was discovered by Guy Mellgren during an excavation of the Native American Goddard archeological site on Naskeag Point in Brooksville in 1957. The tiny silver coin is smaller than a dime.

It was originally thought to be an English coin. Its potential Viking ties were not discovered until 1978. It was minted during the reign of King Olaf III, sometime between 1065 and 1080.

Because no other Viking artifacts were discovered, some researchers believe the coin was merely a trade object that ended up at the Native American village.

Others like to imagine that Vikings did indeed once explore along the coast of Maine and that the coin is proof of that presence. *Maine Atlas: M15, D5*

White Bird Search

A search in Maine for a pair of lost French pilots who may have beat Charles Lindbergh in crossing the Atlantic by eleven days, spawned an organization that continues to search the globe to solve some of aviation's greatest mysteries including the fate of Amelia Earhart and band leader Glenn Miller.

Former Southwest Harbor seasonal resident Richard Gillespie launched a search for the *White Bird*, the plane flown by Charles Nungesser and Francois Coli, after reading an article written by Northeast Harbor horror actor Gunnar Hansen, who starred as Leatherface in *The Texas Chainsaw Massacre*.

Nungesser and Coli left Paris on May 8, 1927. The next day, residents in Washington County, reported hearing an aircraft overhead, a sputtering engine, and the sound of a crash. Reports of hunters finding a massive, twelve-cylinder engine block in the woods years later, helped fuel speculation the aviators were the first to fly nonstop across the Atlantic. Hansen and Gillespie tried several times to find the wreckage of the *White Bird*.

Gillespie went on to found The International Group for Historic Aircraft Recovery (TIGHAR). The effort to find Nungesser and Coli alone spawned 27 TIGHAR expeditions in Maine and Newfoundland. The group has conducted dozens of expeditions to find lost World War II aircraft and has even teamed up with noted oceanographer Robert Ballard, who discovered the wreck of the *Titanic*, in the search for Amelia Earhart. Earhart was the first woman to fly solo across the Atlantic. *Maine Atlas: M26, A2*

Conservancy Preserves Ghost Town's Legacy

Forlorn cellar holes overgrown with trees all across Maine offer testament to earlier settlers, but the Mariaville Falls Preserve along the West Branch of the Union River is the actual site of a thriving town that eventually disappeared entirely.

Often listed as one of the most haunted places in Maine, the preserve was once home to a town that in 1810 sported a dam, two sawmills, a tannery, boarding house, general store, and more than fifty homes.

It was named for Maria, the daughter of Philadelphia investor William Bingham, who owned vast tracts of land in Down East Maine.

As other places flourished, and with farming nearby land difficult, the town only lasted for a few decades. Except for a stone foundation on the west side of the river, nothing of the town, the dam or the mills, remains.

Now owned by the Frenchman Bay Conservancy, there are hiking trails and great spots to view the attractive river, rapids, and falls. Don't worry about ghosts, however. Probably the greatest danger while visiting is not paying attention to the copious patches of poison ivy growing along some of the trails. *Maine Atlas: M24, B2*

Questions Linger Over World War II Blimp Crash

After a US Navy anti-submarine blimp crashed into the Gulf of Maine on the night of July 2, 1944, officials were quick to rule out enemy action.

However, evidence collected after survivors were interviewed and the wreckage retrieved, and testimony from scores of people on shore who offered "ear-witness" testimony, has cast doubt on that theory.

Some details are certain. Earlier that day, two Southwest Harbor lobstermen, Ernest and Merrill Stanley, spotted what appeared to be the periscope of a Nazi submarine in waters near Mount Desert Rock. They reported the sighting after they returned to shore. The 251-foot, helium-filled *K-14* was dispatched from a base in Massachusetts to investigate. Later that evening the blimp's crew failed to check in by radio. The blimp's wreckage was found the next morning. Six of ten crew members perished.

Enemy action was ruled out despite the fact both depth charges were gone and had been dropped in an armed condition. Spent bullet shells littered the gondola floor and the airship's gas bag was riddled with half-inch holes. Lookouts on shore and people in surrounding harbors report hearing explosions and gunfire about the time contact with the airship was lost.

Four months later, German U-boat *1230* dropped a pair of spies ashore at nearby Hancock Point. *Maine Atlas: M16, E5*

Acadia National Park

Acadia National Park sprawls across nearly fifty thousand acres on Mount Desert Island and the Schoodic Peninsula. It was the first park created entirely from donations of private land. Hosting some 3.5 million visitors annually, the park showcases the area's rugged granite shores, deep, cool lakes, verdant forests, and bald mountain tops first spotted by explorer Samuel de Champlain in September of 1604. Created as Sieur de Monts National Monument in 1916, it became Lafayette National Park in 1919 and was renamed Acadia in 1929.

Cadillac Mountain

Cadillac Mountain, at 1,532 feet high, is the tallest mountain within fifty miles of the sea from Maine to Rio de Janeiro. Some days it is the first place touched by the rays of the rising sun in the United States. Atop Cadillac, a mysterious thirteen-inch cross carved into the granite bedrock along the North Ridge Trails has confounded visitors for a century. Legend holds it was chiseled by members of Champlain's crew in 1604. Actually, it is one of four markers delineating the corners of an eighty-nine-acre parcel of land sold to become part of the park. Most likely, they were carved by surveyors around 1908.

Somes Sound

Nearly splitting Mount Desert Island in two, Somes Sound, according to geologists, is not a true fjord because it lacks an oxygen deprived "dead zone" at the bottom. It was downgraded to a "fjard" in 1989. In 2014, area residents dropped a stone tablet into the depths honoring the band, the Grateful Dead, claiming the sound now has a "Dead" zone and is therefore a fjord.

Carriage Roads

After automobiles were first allowed everywhere on the island in 1915, Acadia co-founder John D. Rockefeller Jr., began construction

Opposite (clockwise from top): Bubble Rock in Acadia National Park (*From Author's Collection*); The Cobblestone Bridge on Acadia's Carriage Road system (*From Author's Collection*); Sign at the summit of Penobscot Mountain in Acadia National Park (*From Author's Collection*).

A view of the Cobblestone Bridge along the scenic Carriage Roads of Acadia National Park. *From Author's Collection.*

of a fifty-mile network of carriage roads for walkers and equestrians where motorized travel is prohibited to this day. A total of sixteen unique stone bridges await discovery as part of the system.

Hiking Trails

Acadia has more than one hundred miles of maintained hiking trails, including some with more than one thousand stalwart granite steps. There are fabulous views, mysterious caves, and, on some dangerous trails such as the Precipice, wrought-iron rungs to assist climbers scrambling up sheer granite cliffs.

Sand Beach

Sand Beach is one of Acadia's most popular spots. Mixed with fine sediments are trillions of bits of broken shells. Waves continually sculpt the shore, sometimes revealing the wooden ribs of the shipwrecked schooner *Tar*, usually hidden below the dunes.

Thunder Hole

Thunder Hole is a cleft in the granite shoreline that funnels the power of the Gulf of Maine's massive waves into a narrow area. The water compresses under overhanging rocks and often rockets skyward in a geyser accompanied by a ground-shaking rumble.

Balance Rock

Balance Rock sits atop the South Bubble in the heart of Acadia. It differs from the underlying bedrock however and is believed to have been deposited by a one-mile thick glacier that plucked it from the Dedham area, forty miles to the north. It left this "erratic" behind when it melted.

Sargent Mountain Pond

Sargent Mountain Pond in Acadia is Maine's Oldest Pond. Based on bottom core samples, geologists believe it was the first depression to fill with water as the Laurentide Ice Sheet retreated 16,000 years ago.

Surf's up at Thunder Hole along Ocean Drive in Acadia National Park.
From Author's Collection.

Eastport
Lubec

Eastport and Lubec Live Life On The 'Edge'

Head Down East about as far as you can go and you get to the communities of Eastport and Lubec. While there may be more than a few miles of bad road between there and Machias, the truth is you'll find no better folks in the State of Maine.

A small community composed of several islands, Eastport is the state's least-populous city, having just 1,331 residents in the last census. A center for smuggling during the early 1800s (and during Prohibition), Eastport is the easternmost town in America. This busy modern-day port is known for its once-bustling sardine industry and mustard mill.

Lubec, which was once the epicenter of a major gold swindle, is also the birthplace of Myron Avery, the Mainer who went on to lay out and build much of the storied Appalachian Trail. It is also the jumping-off place for Canada's Campobello Island, located just a tall, arching bridge, and a pair of Customs checkpoints away.

Old Sow Whirlpool

Located northeast off the portion of Eastport on Moose Island, the Old Sow whirlpool is considered the largest in the Western Hemisphere, one of five of its size in the world. Non-motorized vessels and their crews have disappeared into its maw in years gone by. This 250-foot-diameter wonder, is reportedly named for the sucking sound it sometimes makes. Smaller surrounding swirls are known as the "Piglets." Area charter operators will cross Old Sow when conditions are safe.

New Year's Sardine Drop

Eastport has a unique way of celebrating its maritime history and the new year at the same time. For more than fifteen years, a large, illuminated "Great Sardine," is lowered from the third floor of the Tides Institute and Museum of Art building on Bank Square as the

Opposite (clockwise: from top): An early postcard view of the Eastport fishing fleet (*From Author's Collection*); the lighthouse at the nation's easternmost point, Quoddy Head (*From Author's Collection*); President Franklin Delano Roosevelt inspects a scale model of the giant tidal power project planned for Passamaquoddy Bay in 1935. (*Courtesy of Library of Congress*).

seconds count down on Dec. 31. In a nod to the community's close ties to Canada, a giant red maple leaf is lowered at 11 p.m. which is midnight, Atlantic Time.

Easternmost Point in USA

The West Quoddy Point Lighthouse is located on the easternmost point of the continental United States. There has been a lighthouse on the site since 1808.

Although a stone tablet on the grounds of the lighthouse, which is part of Quoddy Head State Park, proclaims the point, the actual easternmost point is on the rocks along the shore at low tide.

Raye's Mustard Mill

Owned by four generations of the same family, Raye's Mustard Mill in Eastport is a working museum, the last facility left in the world to still stone grind mustard seed for the quintessential condiment. It was built in 1903 to provide mustard for the area's many sardine canneries. The mill still makes many wonderful flavors of mustard and tours are available in season.

Campobello Island

Technically in Canada, but inexorably tied to the United States, Campobello Island is the home of Roosevelt Campobello International Park which preserves more than two thousand acres including the thirty-four-room family summer "cottage" of President Franklin Roosevelt. Roosevelt was an ardent supporter of a proposed project using tidal power to make electricity in the region.

Passamaquoddy Tidal Power

The dream of harnessing the power of 140 billion cubic feet of water moving in and out of Passamaquoddy Bay each day (more than moves down the mighty Mississippi River in a week) prompted work

The Roosevelt "Cottage" in the Roosevelt Campobello International Park.
Courtesy of National Park Service.

to begin in the early 1930s. Along with worker villages and other infrastructure, only a few of the planned dams, locks and causeways were built before opposition by electric utilities, congressmen from Southern States, and others scuttled the ambitious plan in 1936.

Designers estimate it would have generated around 342 megawatts of electricity annually.

Reversing Falls

The town of Pembroke is home to a park on Mahar Point from which visitors can observe the famous Reversing Falls, similar to a Class III rapid, created when strong tidal surges twice a day course back and forth over an underwater ledge between Cobscook (Passamaquoddy for "Boiling Water") and Dennys bays.

Things That Go Bump,
Or Howl, in the Night

With ninety percent of the land area covered in forest, Maine is the most heavily forested state in the country. With hundreds of large, often deep, lakes, and an unforgiving coast, there are plenty of places where mythical beasts and creatures can lurk. It seems like nearly every community has its own homegrown legends and mysteries of creatures, both real and imagined, that go bump in the night. The ones on these pages have gotten the most attention over the decades.

Monster of Pocomoonshine Lake

Located far off the beaten path in Washington County, Pocomoonshine Lake is the perfect place for the setting of a lake monster mystery. This one dates back to Native American legends of a forty-foot serpent, as depicted in carved pictographs, followed by a letter in a Machias newspaper in 1882 attempting to refute the existence of the "Chain Lake Snake," after multiple reports of it leaving long, curving tracks on land. Like most good legends, no photos exist. *Maine Atlas: M36, C2*

Wessie the Giant Snake

With no poisonous species remaining in Maine, most folks venturing into the out-of-doors don't worry about snakes. One incident in Westbrook, however, has some reassessing that position. In June 2016, police received reports that a snake, believed to be a giant anaconda more than ten feet long, had been spotted along the Presumpscot River near Riverbank Park. Later, police reportedly saw the snake consuming a large mammal, such as a woodchuck or beaver. In August of that year, a twelve-foot snake skin, believed to be from "Wessie," was found along the riverbank. Biologists said the snake, which was probably raised as a pet and released illegally, was unlikely to have survived its first Maine winter. *Maine Atlas: M74, C2*

Meddybemps Howler

Maine's cousin to Bigfoot is the subject of several stories that tell of large, dark beasts walking erect in the vicinity of remote Meddybemps Lake, a relative stone's throw from Pocomoonshine Lake. The ape-like creatures stand eight feet tall, have reddish hair, and emit a foul odor. Native Americans reportedly still talk of encounters with Gwakcoo, which means "one who is hungry all the time." Their preferred food seems to be the area's abundant freshwater fish, although one tale includes "little girls," among their favorite fare. *Maine Atlas: M36, D4*

Cherryfield Goatman

Back in the 1950s a man in the Cherryfield area reportedly encountered a strange creature after his pickup truck broke down on the remote Blackwoods Road. He described the beast as half-man, half-goat, with the legs of a goat, body of a man, and horns sticking out of his head. Unlike goatmen seen elsewhere in the United States, this one was reportedly wearing a flannel shirt. Without photos it is impossible to ascertain whether the shirt was from Land's End or L.L.Bean. *Maine Atlas: M25, D2*

Fanciful depictions of the Meddybemps Howler, left, and the Cherryfield Goatman. *Courtesy of Wikicommons.*

The Turner Beast

A relative latecomer to mythical creatures in Maine, the Turner Beast was profiled in a newspaper article in August 2006 after terrorizing the region for some fifteen years, although reports go back to 1906. It was described as a 125-pound black predator known for mauling dogs and other pets, and threatening humans. After the *Lewiston Sun Journal* reported the beast had been hit by a car and killed, it sent the DNA away for testing. The test showed it was a very large dog or wolf/dog hybrid. About a year later, a local woman claimed it was her pet. *Maine Atlas: M11, C5*

Cassie the Sea Serpent

Now considered to be Casco Bay's quintessential cryptozoological curiosity, Cassie the Sea Serpent has been spotted on and off for more than two hundred years along the Maine coast from Biddeford to Eastport. Described both as mammal and reptile, it has been estimated to be between 60 and 125 feet long.

Navy officer Edward Preble, who went on to command the USS *Constitution*, reported the first sighting in June 1779 in Penobscot Bay. Other sightings were reported near Portland in 1818, and off Mount Desert Rock in 1836. Reports were filed in 1905 and 1910. The most-detailed sighting was reported by two fishermen, Ole Mikkelsen and Ejmar Hairgaard, in Casco Bay in 1958. *Maine Atlas: M3, A5*

Pamola

Members of the Penobscot Tribe believed that the fearsome god, Pamola, lived in a cave along the precipitous Knife Edge on Katahdin. With the body of a man, head of a moose, and wings and talons of an eagle, the evil Pamola purportedly stood thirty feet high. Early Native American guides reportedly refused to climb above the tree line on the mountain out of fear of being killed and eaten. A famous

A fanciful sea monster detail from an early map of the Gulf of Maine.
Courtesy of Library of Congress.

painting by Damariscotta artist Maurice Jake Day shows a more benevolent Pamola sharing stories with legendary Baxter State Park Ranger Leroy Dudley. *Maine Atlas: M51, D1*

The Basin Screecher

Eerie, shrill cries coming from a wilderness known as the basin in the coastal town of Phippsburg have been variously attributed over the decades to owls, foxes, raccoons, or the spirits of murdered children. One blogger reports seeing the source of the noises coming from a "small, quadrupedal animal."

In 2019, three local teenagers produced a video called "The Hunt for the Basin Screecher." They attribute the noises to a "half-man, half-bird cryptoid." Of course, no photos of the creature are known to exist. *Maine Atlas: M6, D4*

Midcoast

Midcoast

At the turn of the seventeenth century, both French and English explorers were drawn to the mystery and possibilities of the Maine coast. Today, there's plenty to see and do beyond eating at the ubiquitous lobster pounds and shopping at trendy gift stores and galleries that cater to tourists.

On the village green in Thomaston, the Weymouth Boulder commemorates the explorations of adventurer George Weymouth who visited on the wings of his vessel *Archangel* in 1605. Nearby is a bizarre granite obelisk on the lawn of a gadfly writer known as the Humble Farmer. It claims to mark the "Center of the Universe." Can you prove him wrong?

Rockland has experienced a renaissance in recent years with new gourmet restaurants and an expanded Farnsworth Art Museum, featuring its connections to Maine's First Family of Art, the Wyeths. Here, too, you'll find the birthplace of poet Edna St. Vincent Millay whose poem "Renascence," describes the view of picturesque Camden from Mount Battie and navigates the depths of the universe of the heart.

Farther down the coast, Damariscotta plays host to the annual Pumpkinfest and is also the birthplace of Maine's homespun retail chain, Reny's.

Previous page, (clockwise from top): An engraving of Captain George Weymouth making contact with Native Americans in 1605, (*Courtesy of Wikicommons*); "Lighthouse Heroine" Abbie Burgess, (*Courtesy of Digicommons*); the Frances Perkins Homestead in Newcastle (*Courtesy of the Perkins Center*); and the Humble Farmer's Center of the Universe marker in St. George (*From Author's Collection*).

Heroine Kept Beacon Blazing

Perhaps no one better epitomizes the hardy and resolute nature of coastal Mainers than young Abbie Burgess who became known as the "Lighthouse Heroine."

Abbie Burgess.
Courtesy of Wikicommons.

Born in Rockland in 1839, the same year a massive storm destroyed the first wooden tower lighthouses erected on remote Matinicus Rock, Abbie was the fourth child of Samuel and Thankful Burgess. Her father became tender of the rebuilt twin, ninety-foot, granite lighthouses on a treeless rock more than twenty miles offshore in 1853. By the time she was a teenager, she helped operate the whale oil-fired beacons and two-thousand-pound fog bell.

In January 1859, nearly two months after a supply boat failed to arrive, Samuel Burgess sailed and rowed twenty-five miles to Rockland for supplies. Because Thankful Burgess was an invalid at this point, 17-year-old Abbie was in charge. After Samuel left, an enormous gale blew in, sending waves crashing completely over the thirty-two-acre island and forcing the family to seek refuge in the cramped north tower. Even though the storm abated after five days, high waves delayed Samuel's return for three more weeks. Throughout that time, Abbie kept the lights burning, and, despite meager rations, tended to her mother and her younger siblings.

Abbie later married a lighthouse keeper. She died in 1892 at the age of 52. A tiny lighthouse helps identify her grave in the Forest Hills Cemetery in South Thomaston. In 1998, the US Coast Guard commissioned the 175-foot buoy tender *Abbie Burgess* in her honor. It is stationed in Rockland. *Maine Atlas: M9, D1*

Harry Goodridge and his famous Rockport "Sea Dog," Andre the Seal.
Courtesy of Digicommons.

Sea Dog was Man's Best Friend

When it comes to being a Maine man's best friend, it's hard not to think of Rockport's most famous "Sea Dog," Andre.

Immortalized in books, newspapers, and films, Andre the Seal was found, purportedly abandoned, on Robinson's Rock in Penobscot Bay in May 1961. He was adopted by local harbormaster Harry Goodridge, who envisioned him as a scuba diving partner who would soon return to the wild on his own—but the seal never did.

Andre spent time with the Goodridge family, watching television with the kids, and luxuriating in the bathtub. Harry taught him how to shake hands and cover his eyes with his flippers. Feeding time at the harbor became a time-honored tourist attraction nearly every day from April until November. In winter, as the harbor iced over, Andre would disappear, only to return each spring.

Eventually Goodridge began driving Andre to either the New England

Aquarium in Boston, or the Mystic Aquarium in Connecticut for the winter. Each spring, Harry would return to the aquarium, take Andre to a nearby beach, and release him. And like clockwork, several days, or a couple weeks, later, Andre would magically reappear in Rockport.

Andre, who was believed to be the oldest living wild harbor seal, spent twenty-five summers with Goodridge until he died in 1986. Goodridge passed away in 1990.

A memorial statue created by sculptor Jane Wasey honoring Andre is now located in a park on the Rockport waterfront. *Maine Atlas: M79, C1*

Southport Home to Wicked Witch of the West

While Maine may never have put witches on trial or burned them at the stake, at least one cinematic sorceress, as well as her little dog, can be counted among the state's list of leading summer residents.

Margaret Hamilton, who frightened generations of small children with a threat of "I'll get you, my pretty!" as the Wicked Witch of the West in *The Wizard of Oz,* spent her downtime in her house on Cape Island, off the village of Cape Newagen, which is in Southport. Hamilton and her family followed her personal yellow brick road to

Margaret Hamilton, who played the Wicked Witch of the West" in *The Wizard of Oz,* owned a summer home near Boothbay Harbor.
Courtesy of Wikicommons.

Maine and purchased the retreat in 1961. No legions of flying monkeys ever appeared and Hamilton was well-liked by area residents. She could frequently be seen rowing the short distance between the town pier and her private dock on what area residents affectionately called "Witches Island."

Hamilton starred in the fantasy classic in 1939. In it, her character is defeated when water is thrown on her and she melts. While in Maine, she had a frightening moment when water almost brought about her demise in real life.

According to Bass Harbor writer Laurie Schreiber, Hamilton fell into the cold autumn water off a ladder at the town dock one day after rowing from the island and, if not for an alert taxi driver, could have foundered and drowned.

Hamilton died in 1985. Her family continues to enjoy the island today. *Maine Atlas: M7, D2*

Crash Creates Controversial Corner

In a state where varnished moose turds are sold to tourists as jewelry, there's no shortage of people who can be suspected of being full of you-know-what. But no place touts its scatological claim to fame with as much gusto, or pride, as one sharp turn in the road in Lincoln County.

A sign on a tall post located at Larry Russell's dairy farm along Route 196 in Newcastle demarks Cowshit Corner. Legend holds that the corner got its name when rain washed cow manure from a roadside barn onto the pavement, causing a mail truck to slide off the road and hit a utility pole. Soon after, a sign appeared that read "Cowshit Corner, slippery when wet."

The name, well, has stuck.

The sign itself has changed over the years and now says "Welcome to . . . " The corner has been the subject of numerous network news

Maine's most infamous corner in Newcastle.
Courtesy of Wanda Wilcox.

reports and even spawned a short-lived reality local cable TV show. While never in danger of upstaging *Duck Dynasty* in a ratings war, it featured a cast of local characters throwing the bull at the "Church of the Holy Cow."

Cowshit Corner floats have been entered in area parades and, in an attempt to "spread it around," it even has its own YouTube, Facebook and online merchandise sites. *Maine Atlas: M13, E3*

Circus Ship Fire Sparks Legends

The tale of Maine's famous "Circus Ship," which went down in flames in the fall of 1836, has all the elements necessary for a great maritime disaster story—lost treasure, tragedy, and triumph.

The 164-foot steamship *Royal Tar* left Eastport on October 21 with seventy-two passengers and twenty-one crew headed for Portland. Also on board were an elephant, camels, horses, and other animals that were part of Burgess and Dexter's Zoological Institute, a traveling circus. The steamer struggled to make its way down the coast in adverse weather.

On the afternoon of October 25, fire broke out on the ship when it was just off the Fox Islands in Penobscot Bay. Suppression efforts failed. Unfortunately, two of the vessel's four lifeboats were taken off in Eastport to make room for circus equipment, which made abandoning ship difficult.

Many passengers were forced to jump into the sea. The animals were released "in hopes they reach shore." A nearby revenue cutter helped rescue survivors. Others made it in a small boat to Isle au Haut.

In all, thirty-two people were lost and every animal, except for two horses, perished.

The exact location of the final sinking is unknown as the burning hull drifted out to sea. According to reports, the ship's safe, containing gold and silver coins and cash, went down with the wreck. In an ironic twist, Capt. Thomas Reed learned several days later that his son had died on the same day as the sinking.

The plight of the *Royal Tar* inspired children's book illustrator Chris Van Dusen to put out the book *Circus Ship*, but in his story the vessel runs aground and the animals and humans escape serious harm. *Maine Atlas: M15, E2*

Oysters Lured Tribes to Coast

While modern-day Damariscotta is well known for its annual Pumpkinfest and Regatta featuring great food, pumpkin smashing, and a giant pumpkin race in the harbor (people hollow out pumpkins and use them as vessels), it was another gastrological delight that first put the area on the metaphorical map some 2,200 years ago.

Early European settlers were amazed to discover gigantic mounds of oyster shells, called middens, left behind by Native Americans who archeologists believe frequented the area some twenty centuries earlier. While many shell mounds around the country cover a few square yards and are maybe a foot or two deep, the Whalesback Midden in Damariscotta once covered eleven acres, was more than a quarter mile long, and may have been thirty-feet deep at one time. Some of the shells discovered were unusually large, bigger than a person's hand. Bones of deer and fish, as well as pottery shards and some stone implements have also been found. There are eleven middens in the area.

It is believed they were deposited by several tribes who visited the area in late winter and spring over more than a thousand years. The site on the east side of the river was named the Whalesback because the shape reminded people of the marine mammals. In the late 1800s, it was heavily mined for the calcium carbonate content which was manufactured into chicken feed. It is now only a fraction of its original size. It became a state historic site in 2005.

Directly across the river in Newcastle, the Glidden site, the largest remaining in the United States, remains untouched although it is threatened by rising sea levels.

While oysters were nowhere to be found in the river when the first European settlers arrived, they are there now, raised in the floating cages of enterprising oyster farmers that have returned the tasty shellfish to regional tables. *Maine Atlas: M7, A3*

Perkins was Real Deal for Workers

President Franklin Roosevelt may get most of the credit for lifting the nation out of the Great Depression and creating the Civilian Conservation Corps, Public Works Administration, minimum wage, forty-hour workweek, and Social Security, but it was a woman with ties to Maine who actually helped make all those things possible. Frances Perkins, a woman with family roots from midcoast Maine (her mother was from Bethel, her dad from Newcastle), promoted the New Deal.

Frances Perkins, architect of Social Security and other worker protections, with President Franklin D. Roosevelt. *Courtesy of Perkins Center.*

Perkins, Roosevelt's Labor Secretary, was the first female Cabinet Officer in United States history. She made a presidential promise to pursue all goals of the New Deal a condition to taking the job. The only item not finished: Universal Health Care.

After government service, she enjoyed a life of teaching and scholarship at Cornell University.

She spent many summers throughout her life at the family home in Maine. Founded in 2008, the Frances Perkins Center looks to preserve her legacy and the Perkins family homestead, built in 1837 along the Damariscotta River. On January 3, 2020, the center—which offers tours and holds events—purchased the home, which is on the National Register of Historic Places.

Perkins is buried in Glidden Cemetery in Newcastle. *Maine Atlas: M7, A3*

Ancient Stones Prompt Spirited Debate

The possibility that Vikings visited the Maine coast long before Columbus has captured the popular imagination here for generations. So it was no surprise back in 1971, when Walter Elliott Jr. claimed to

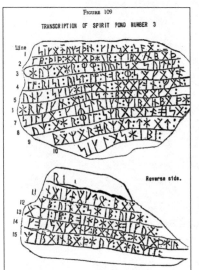

have discovered three stones covered in Old Norse runes near Spirit Pond in Phippsburg, that the find received great publicity.

Two stones reportedly have text carved into them and one is a map. One amateur archeologist has even suggested the map shows the landscape as viewed from the top of the White Mountains in New Hampshire. Others believe it shows the mouth of the Kennebec River.

Spirit Pond drawings.
Courtesy of Digicommons.

In 1974, a Harvard researcher announced that the stones contained only "a few Norse words in a sea of gibberish." Carbon 14 dating of charcoal found during a subsequent excavation near the spot where the stones were found supposedly dates from the 1400s. The most outlandish theories involve the stones originating with the Knights Templar and that they refer to the Holy Grail.

Over the years, debate has swirled over the stones' authenticity, with most mainstream scholars believing they are fakes. But that view is not universal. The stones now reside at the Maine State Museum in Augusta.

Today, you can hike on trails in the Spirit Pond Preserve on the north side of the tidal pond. *Maine Atlas: M6, E5*

A Not-So-Humble Monument

Geographers are always fascinated with finding the center of things, but there's no question the jury is still out about where the center of the universe is located. One resident of St. George, however, has no doubt and has erected a sixteen-foot obelisk on his lawn declaring his dooryard to be exactly that.

Robert Skoglund, a newspaper columnist, humorist, radio commentator, and gadfly topped the granite finger with a five-foot, sheet-steel monkey blowing a horn. It helps guide people to the Humble Farmer Bed and Breakfast that he and his wife, Marsha, "the almost perfect woman," operate along the River Road.

Skoglund, who likes to brag he sold rhubarb to pay for the inn's solar panels, produced an evening radio show on Maine Public Broadcasting for twenty-eight years. His columns appeared in many Maine weekly and daily papers.

According to Google, the Center of the Universe is someplace in Tulsa, Oklahoma. But most physicists agree there is no actual center because every place in it began expanding equally at the Big Bang. So who is to say it's not in the middle of your front lawn? *Maine Atlas: M8, A2*

Island's Organ Returns After Century

The story of fabled Hurricane Island in Penobscot Bay is one of settlement, abandonment, and eventual reuse.

Gen. Davis Tillson, who lost a foot in an accident at West Point, bought the island in 1870 with the idea of quarrying its distinctive pink-gray granite. A community of hundreds soon sprang up with stonecutters flocking to the 125-acre island from Italy, Ireland, Sweden, and Finland. Soon the school had sixty students and the island's population soared to 250 people. Tillson keep tight control and prohibited alcohol, although some reports say a bootlegger vessel, the *Dark Secret*, was known to anchor offshore. Stone from Hurricane Island made its way into scores of projects including the Brooklyn Bridge and Washington Monument.

Then, the town closed almost overnight in 1914 leaving a ghost town behind. Eventually, a Story and Clark pump organ was removed from the abandoned Catholic church on the island and moved to North Haven. From 1964 to 2006 the island was used by the Hurricane Island Outward Bound School.

In 2009, it was taken over by the Hurricane Island Center for Science and Leadership, which operates a small, off-the-grid, research station. In 2016, the Center recovered the organ from the now-closed church on North Haven, returned it to Hurricane, repaired it, and it now provides music regularly in the groups galley. *Maine Atlas: M9, A1*

Island Evictions Still a Point of Shame

Located at the mouth of the New Meadows River in Phippsburg, forty-two-acre Malaga Island tells the story of an erstwhile settlement of economically disadvantaged minorities and social outcasts

Residents of Malaga Island, who were uprooted and moved by the state in the early 1900s. *Courtesy of Peter Roberts.*

and their struggles to live during a time of social and political rigidity and intolerance.

A mixed-race community developed on the island just after the Civil War. In addition to a worsening economy, the island's residents ran afoul of the growing eugenics movement which held that the poor, criminal, or those society deemed immoral, were the result of heredity. Despite efforts by missionaries to help, including building a school and other assistance, the island's higher profile resulted in unflattering articles such as one titled "Queer Folk of the Maine Coast."

Malaga residents were declared wards of the state in 1905 and in 1912 the state purchased the island from its owner and evicted everyone. A few remaining buildings were burned.

Even seventeen bodies in the island graveyard were placed into five caskets and moved to a plot at the Maine School for the Feeble Minded (now Pineland Farms in New Gloucester) where eight residents had been involuntarily committed a year earlier.

In 2010, government officials apologized. A memorial was erected at Pineland's Cemetery in 2017. Malaga Island is now protected by the Maine Coast Heritage Trust. *Maine Atlas: M6, D4*

Gardens Aglow at This Botanical Gem

When people think of gardens, most picture them in summertime, but winter is when this botanical gem really shines.

The Coastal Maine Botanical Gardens in Boothbay, which has been named the number one garden in America by TripAdvisor, really does it up right for the darkest time of the year—decorating its trees, structures and paths with more than 650,000 energy-efficient LED lights.

The display, which runs from mid-November to New Year's Eve, is open nightly until 9 p.m. There is an admission charge. Because of its popularity, advanced reservations are recommended. Tickets are sold in advance and regularly sell out. In 2018, nearly 100,000 people took in the display. Nightly caps were put in place in 2019 to improve the visitor experience.

The fourteen-acre light display area is only a small portion of the 295-acre Botanical Garden preserve, the largest in New England. Opened in 2007, it includes seventeen acres featuring plants indigenous to Maine and northern climates. The property includes shoreside walking paths and a meditation garden. *Maine Atlas: M7, C2*

Cemetery Features Best, Worst Examples in Child Care

One of the saddest events in Midcoast Maine history was the discovery of a naked body of a five-month-old baby boy floating in water at the bottom of a Rockport lime quarry, near the town dump, on April 20, 1940.

Authorities determined the baby was already dead when it was put in the water. No cause could ever be determined. Birth records were checked and a $500 reward—the equivalent of nearly $10,000 today—was offered, but no leads were found and the body remained unclaimed.

Touched by the little boy's plight, people donated money to give him a proper burial in the Seaview Cemetery on Warrenton Street. A simple stone marks the spot. Caretakers frequently find toys, coins, stuffed animals, and other mementos at the grave site.

Ironically, in the same cemetery lies the grave of one of the world's foremost child care experts, pediatrician Benjamin Spock. In 1946, he wrote the *Common Sense Book of Baby and Child Care*, which became the definitive source on raising children during the 1950s, 1960s, 1970s, and beyond. More than fifty million copies have been sold. Dr. Spock, as he was known, had a house in Camden and loved to sail his boat *Turtle*. He died in 1988. *Maine Atlas: M14, E3*

Weymouth Voyage Left Large Wake

The exploits of English explorer Captain George Weymouth who visited Monhegan and named the St. George River (after St. George) in Thomaston, continue to reverberate along the Maine coast to this day.

He arrived in the spring of 1605 and explored the river as well as places in present-day Thomaston and Cushing. The purpose of the voyage was to establish a colony in Virginia. Weymouth had spent time in Canadian waters three years earlier looking for the Northwest Passage. A cross at the Thomaston Town Landing marks the spot where the first Englishman is believed to have set foot in North America.

On the three hundredth anniversary of Weymouth's visit, more than two thousand people turned out to dedicate a boulder with a plaque memorializing Weymouth's achievements on the village green in Thomaston. A stone cross was also erected on Allen Island just off-shore where Weymouth is believed to have anchored in his vessel *Archangel*. That island is now owned by the family of artist Andrew Wyeth.

When returning to England, Weymouth took along five kidnapped Native Americans. Legend holds that among them was a man named Squanto, who several years later, after receiving an education and learning English, managed to get back to America and greet the Pilgrims in their own language when they arrived in 1620.

While Squanto was kidnapped by Europeans and did learn English, there's no evidence it was Weymouth's party that was responsible, researchers note. *Maine Atlas: M8, A2*

Plaster or Bronze, Statue Honors Lobstermen

The bronze Lobsterman's Memorial at Land's End on Bailey Island is one of three based on an original plaster model that once graced the 1939 World's Fair in New York.

Crafted by sculptor Victor Kahill of Portland, it was a likeness of lobsterman H. Elroy "Snoody" Johnson of Bailey Island. Because a private fundraising effort did not come up with enough money to cast Snoody in bronze, Kahill painted the plaster model with bronze paint and it went on display anyway.

Hermit of Manana

Maine has no shortage of hermits ranging from the modern-day North Pond Hermit to the Hermit of Monson, to the well-publicized Maine Hermit, who was a roadside attraction in Freeport during the 1930s.

But perhaps the most forlorn hermit story belongs to Ray Phillips, who sailed into the sheltered harbor at Monhegan in 1931 and lived a solitary existence until his death at age 83 in 1974.

Phillips worked as a fisherman for a time on Monhegan before buying a small lot and

The fact the statue didn't include the fisherman's trusty dog Bruin, who helped separate "keepers" from "shorts" on Snoody's boat, turned into a minor kerfuffle. To soothe feelings, the commissioner of Maine's Sea and Shore Fisheries Department presented the dog his own lobster fishing license at the statue's unveiling at the World's Fair.

Some thirty-five years later, after the state approved funding, Boothbay artist Norman Therrien fixed the original and cast three bronze copies comprised of seventeen different pieces. One remains on display at Lobsterman Park at 1 Temple Street in Portland, one can be found outside the Land's End Gift Shop, and one—originally in the lobby of the Maine State Library in Augusta—is now in Washington, D.C.

The 800-pound, seven-foot-tall statue on Bailey Island is located literally where Route 24 ends at the edge of the sea. *Maine Atlas: M6, E2*

House Preserves, Protects Poet's Legacy

The house where the celebrated poet Edna St. Vincent Millay was born on Broadway in Rockland is now owed by a nonprofit that is

setting up on treeless Manana Island just across the harbor from the main wharf on Monhegan. Except for an historic US Coast Guard fog signaling station, there are only one or two other structures on the island, which also won notoriety for carved stone runes at times ascribed to the Vikings, Celts, or Phoenicians. The island, located about ten miles offshore, is barely half a mile wide and three-quarters of a mile long.

Born in 1892, Phillips grew up in Newport, Maine, and later attended the University of Maine, fought in World War I and lived for a time in New York City where he worked as a food inspector. His home on Manana was a twelve-by-fifteen-foot shack made of driftwood. He kept a large goose as a pet, which he referred to as his "watchdog." His ashes were buried on Manana.

A short film about Phillips, *The Hermit of Manana*, was released in 2006. *Maine Atlas: M8, D1*

Ray Phillips, the Hermit of Manana. *Courtesy of Digicommons.*

Edna St. Vincent Millay.
Courtesy of Library of Congress.

developing it as an educational hub, writers' retreat and place to learn more about the writer famous for, among other things, the following lines: "My candle burns at both ends; it will not last the night; but ah, my foes, and oh, my friends—it gives a lovely light!"

Efforts to preserve the location are nearly a century old. In 1934, the Rockland Women's Educational Club placed a wooden commemorative marker on the house.

Millay, a playwright and activist, grew up in Camden. She won the Pulitzer Prize for Poetry in 1915.

The house is now in the process of being restored by the nonprofit Millay House Rockland, which also sponsors an annual Millay Arts and Poetry Festival. The group purchased the house from the Rockland Historical Society in 2017. *Maine Atlas: M79, B2*

Tallest Trap Tree a Town Tradition

Inventive Mainers are often repurposing everyday objects to help celebrate the holidays. And nowhere is there a better example than Rockland's lobster trap tree that goes up every November at Harbor Park.

The forty-foot-tall tree, believed to be the world's tallest, must be carefully constructed to insure safety. It features 155 wire-mesh lobster traps that are all interconnected with plastic zip ties. All the work is done by volunteers including members of the US Coast Guard and work release jail inmates. The finished product is decorated with more than 2,500 lights, 600 feet of garland, and 100 actual lobster buoys.

The tree becomes the centerpiece of the community's long-running Festival of Lights. The tree lighting ceremony is traditionally the Friday night after Thanksgiving.

When the tree is disassembled, some of the traps are raffled off.

Other places install similar creations including a tree made of wooden lobster storage crates at the Trenton Bridge Lobster Pound in Trenton, and lobster trap trees in Jonesport, York, Kennebunkport, Portland, and Ogunquit.

Harbor Park, which is also home to the town's annual Maine Lobster Festival, also sports the world's largest lobster cooker, capable of preparing 1,600 pounds of steamed lobsters in just 15 minutes. *Maine Atlas: M79, B2*

Winter Ice Meant Hard, Cold Cash

Maine's legendary winters produced an abundance of ice and during the mid- to late-1800s entrepreneurs from Kittery to Eastport were doing a brisk business selling large blocks of ice to vendors in big cities and throughout the Caribbean. By 1880, more than 1,500 vessels were employed in transporting ice just from the Kennebec River alone.

Cutters used handsaws, and later mechanized gear, to make deep slits in the ice on frozen lakes and ponds. Blocks were cut to a standard size and stored in wooden buildings that often used sawdust for insulation. Some was stored and sold locally throughout the year. Others were shipped out on schooners, especially where the blocks could be sluiced directly from the lake or pond to docks on ice-free ocean water.

You can discover more about Maine's ice industry today at the Thompson Ice House, the last remaining commercial icehouse in Maine, on Route 129 in Bristol. It was placed on the National Register of Historic Places in 1974. Asa Thompson built a dam at the outlet of a small pond in 1826 and began harvesting ice. In 1987 the pond and icehouse were deeded to a nonprofit group, The Thompson Ice House Preservation Corporation. The group operates a museum and demonstrates harvesting techniques in winter. *Maine Atlas: M7, C3*

Shipbuilding Tradition Strong as Steel

The tradition of shipbuilding near Bath goes back some four hundred years to the earliest colonists at Popham Beach who built the first sailing ship in the New World, the pinnace *Virginia* in 1607, thirteen years before the arrival of the *Mayflower*. An ample supply of timber and the industrious nature of early settlers combined to give birth to a growing industry. The first four-masted schooner was built in Bath in 1880. And soon after, Bath native Gen. Thomas Hyde founded Bath Iron Works in 1884.

Along with commercial and fishing vessels, lightships, and yachts such as the America's Cup defender *Ranger*, and working boats such as the steamship *Katahdin* at Moosehead Lake, the yard specialized in work for the US Navy, producing the then-fastest battleship *Georgia* in 1904.

The yard expanded steadily during World War I and World War II—when it was launching a destroyer every seventeen days. Sailors coined the phrase "Bath-built is best-built." The yard's giant crane, has towered over the town and Kennebec River since 1973.

Since 1995, Bath Iron Works has been a subsidiary of defense contracting giant General Dynamics. It employs more than 6,500 people.

In recent years the yard has focused on building, retrofitting and repairing *Arleigh Burke*-class destroyers, and three advanced *Zumwalt*-class destroyers. *Maine Atlas: M6, C5*

Echoes of Stowe's 'Pearl' Exist Today

Published a decade after her most-famous work, *Uncle Tom's Cabin*, Harriet Beecher Stowe's *The Pearl of Orr's Island*, provided an intimate look at life in the small fishing village of Harpswell at the onset of the Civil War. Stowe, who lived in the town of Brunswick, worked on the book for more than a decade. *Pearl* did not garner the same attention as *Uncle Tom's Cabin*. Maine writer Sara Orne Jewett damned the book with faint praise saying it "has a divine touch here and there in an incomplete piece of work."

The dwelling where Stowe's character, Mara (Pearl) lives actually exists and was known in those days as the Pennel House. After the book came out, it became known as the "Pearl House" and appeared in numerous engravings and on postcards. Both Pearl House, and a seaside grotto where a pair of characters become trapped by the tide, still exist.

Stowe's house at 63 Federal Street in Brunswick, where it is believed she worked on *Uncle Tom's Cabin* and other manuscripts, is now owned

A postcard image celebrating writer Harriet Beecher Stowe's book, "The Pearl of Orr's Island." *From Author's Collection.*

by Bowdoin College. A room where Stowe wrote is open to the public. Decades earlier, Henry Wadsworth Longfellow rented a room in the same house when he was a student at Bowdoin. *Maine Atlas: M6, D3*

Fleet Commander His Own Worst Enemy

It wasn't until Pearl Harbor that the United States suffered a worse naval defeat than it experienced during the Penobscot Expedition in Penobscot Bay in 1779. A total of forty-four ships and 1,000 troops, including an artillery unit commanded by Paul Revere himself, left Boston on July 19, 1779, with plans to attack the British garrison and its three warships and a hastily built Fort George at present-day Castine on the banks of the Bagaduce River. The American forces conducted minimal operations for three weeks allowing British reinforcements to arrive. Despite his fleet's superior firepower, American overall commander Dudley Saltonstall ordered his ships to flee upriver toward present-day Bangor when British relief warships attacked. All the American ships were driven ashore or burned or scuttled and sunk. Survivors fled overland with few provisions.

Saltonstall, whose descendants included the beloved 55th governor of Massachusetts, Leverett A. Saltonstall, was court-martialed because the defeat and was placed on "a want of proper Spirit and Energy on the part of the Commodore." Revere was acquitted of any wrongdoing.

On the two hundredth anniversary in 1979, a Saltonstall relative noted "there's no question my ancestor behaved quite badly." *Maine Atlas: M15, B2*

Soggy Center Inspires Hole-y Doughnut

Whether you run best on Dunkin' or get your morning lift at Tim Hortons, the basic design of today's classic doughnut with a hole in the middle points back to Rockport.

Serving as a crewman on a schooner hauling lime in 1847, 16-year-old Hanson Gregory was not satisfied with the square and diamond-shaped fried cakes of the day that tended to be raw in the middle when done around the edges. According to an interview in *The Washington Post* in 1916, when he was 74, Capt. Gregory explained "I took the cover off the ship's tin pepper box, and—I cut into the middle of that donut the first hole ever seen by mortal eyes!" Later, he had a tinsmith make a special cutter and shared copies with friends and relatives, including his mother Mary who helped spread the word.

Legend holds that Capt. Gregory once took advantage of his hole-y doughnuts to store several on the handles of his ship's wheel to leave both hands free for navigation. Capt. Gregory died in 1921. In 1940, the World's Fair in New York had an exhibit about doughnuts and included a portrait of Gregory.

On the one hundredth anniversary of Capt. Gregory's discovery, a stone marker and plaque commemorating it was placed at 179 Old County Road in Rockport near the current Lutheran Church. *Maine Atlas: M14, E3*

Camden

Camden by the Sea Has Plenty to See

Camden occupies a special place in the pantheon of picturesque Maine harbors. It really does have it all—tall ships at anchor, an island lighthouse standing guard at entrance, bustling downtown village with shops and restaurants, and the mountains of Camden Hills State Park looming behind it all—the capstone to the quintessential Mountains-to-the-Sea community.

It was here that Pulitzer Prize-winning poet Edna St. Vincent Millay first put pen to paper and where, in 1912 at age 20, she wrote "Renascence," which opens: "All I could see from where I stood, Was three long mountains and a wood; I turned and looked another way, And saw three islands in a bay."

While, for some, Camden is second only to Wiscasset for Route 1 traffic backups in summer, those willing to look beyond the commuter inconveniences will find the place has quite a story to tell.

Town Becomes Peyton Place

Based on the best-selling book of the same name, the movie *Peyton Place*, was filmed in Camden and Belfast in 1957. Because of the book's then-racy content, the local library didn't even have the book on its shelves. During a month of filming by 20th Century Fox, more than five hundred residents were hired as "extras." Locations included the Whitehall Inn, Mount Battie, the library amphitheater, and private homes and businesses.

Norumbega Castle Overlooks Sea

Built in 1886 for inventor Joseph Barker Stearns of Weld, Norumbega Castle is located just north of the village on US Route 1. Rising three stories high, the Victorian stone and timber mansion was placed on the National Register of Historic Places in 1974. It was advanced for its time, boasting steam heat and electric lights. The structure, which

Opposite (top to bottom): Schooner *George M. Wells*, rigged and ready to sail from Camden (*Courtesy of Digicommons*); A group of picnickers gathers around the base of the stone tower on Mount Battie in Camden. (*Courtesy of Digicommons.*)

in the past has counted former Assistant Secretary of State Hodding Carter III among its owners, is now used as an inn.

Balance Rock Defies Gravity

Located in the Nature Conservancy's Fernald's Neck Preserve on Megunticook Lake, Camden's Balance Rock is actually in the village of Lincolnville. The solid granite glacial erratic, which appears to be balanced on its tip, has been a popular hiking destination for more than a century.

Maiden's Cliff Memorializes Tragedy

Maiden's Cliff on Mount Megunticook in Camden Hills State Park sports a large cross, visible for miles, high on the cliff where 11-year-old Elenora French fell three hundred feet to her death in 1864. Some believe her spirit continues to haunt the spot, where a white mist frequently lingers, to this day. Because of damage and vandalism, the current cross is not the original.

Tower Holds Mystery

The latest structure atop Mount Battie is a twenty-six-foot-high stone tower memorializing World War I. The tower, accessible via road from Camden Hills State Park, was built in 1921 and was designed as a replica of a tower in Newport, Rhode Island, purported to have been of Viking origin. In 1923, the KKK burned a cross atop the mountain. A star of lights is erected on it each Christmas.

Camden Toboggan Nationals and Chute

While modest by ski mountain standards, the Camden Snow Bowl is most famous for its Jack Williams Toboggan Chute that shoots sleds out onto frozen Hosmer Pond. The ice-covered, wooden structure is some four hundred feet long. It is open to the public, conditions

Opposite: The grand estate Norumbega in Camden was built as a private home and is now in use as an inn. *Courtesy of Digicommons.*

permitting, for an hourly fee. Each February the US National Toboggan Championships are held at the Snow Bowl with many teams sporting catchy names and outlandish costumes.

Home of the Six-Masted Schooner

In the race to make ever-larger sailing ships, Waldoboro gained fame as home to the five-masted schooner. Camden, however, one-upped that, being the home of the world's first six-masted ship in 1900. The 325-foot *George M. Wells* was built at the Holly M. Bean shipyard. Some 10,000 people watched the launch. It wrecked on Ocracoke Island in North Carolina in 1913. The children of its namesake went on to create Sturbridge Village in Massachusetts.

Lobster Lore

- Maine has more than 4,500 licensed lobstermen and -women. Collectively they fish about three million traps.

- A female lobster lays anywhere from several thousand to 100,000 eggs at a time, but only one-tenth of one percent of those eggs will develop and live past six weeks in the larva stage.

- It takes a lobster four to seven years to grow to be one pound in weight.

- The largest known lobster caught in Maine measured forty inches from the rostrum (back) to the end of the tail and weighed twenty-seven pounds. It was caught by a dragger fisherman in 2012 and later returned to the sea. One of the largest known ever caught is a forty-four-pound monster on display (dead and mounted) at the Museum of Science in Boston.

- A lobster can be right-handed or left-handed, meaning some have the large crusher on the left, others on the right.

- A lobster can drop a claw as a defense mechanism and grow another over a period of years.

- An adult male lobster will grow a new shell and shed its old one about once a year, females once every two years, increasing an average of one-half inch and one-third pound with each molt. During its early growth stages, a lobster is believed to shed some twenty-five times over five to seven years.

After a molt, a lobster's shell takes about eight weeks to harden.

 Maine coastal waters provided 119 million pounds of lobsters in 2018, worth nearly $500 million. Conservation efforts include minimum and maximum size limits, escape vents in traps, and not keeping egg-bearing females. In the 1800s, lobsters sometimes washed up on shore after large storms. Because they were not considered fit to eat, they were put into compost piles, or sometimes served to the hired help.

 Maine lobsters are typically depicted as red, but that's only after they are cooked. In the wild, they are a dull, greenish brown with some spots of yellow. However, sometimes special lobsters appear including blue, yellow, and calico ones (1 in 30 million), red ones, white ones, and some that are dual colors with the pigment split right down the middle. The odds of finding a black/orange lobster are 1 in 50 million. Only 1 in 100 million lobsters are thought to be albino.

P. BAXTER'S
PET
CEMETERY

Southern
Maine

Southern Maine Coast

Maine's first settlement may have been farther down the coast, but it is in Southern Maine where things really took root. Falling water along the Saco River in Biddeford powered industrious settlers to contribute the sound of sawmills to the trackless forests of Maine. Along with bragging rights to the nation's first sawmill, York County was also home to the state's first jail.

Portland is Maine's largest city and despite its urban vibe is home to the Cryptozoology Museum, which pays homage to creatures somewhat real and completely imagined. On Mackworth Island, the late Governor Percival Baxter created a private "pet cemetery," for the graves of his horses and Irish setters.

Portland is where the world's chewing gum industry began and was home to Neal Dow, "Father of Prohibition." The town that once rioted over rum, now sports some seventeen microbreweries eager to slake the thirst of modern-day explorers.

There is no question Portland is number one when it comes to triumph over adversity, surviving destruction by the British in the War of 1812, a naval excursion by a Confederate Raider during the Civil War, and the devastating fire of 1866 that destroyed more than six hundred buildings.

Freeport is the state's shopping mecca, a place where L.L.Bean serves as a sprawling temple to blaze orange and plaid. Next door, in Yarmouth, you can circle the planet in the atrium lobby of Garmin, which is home to Eartha, the world's largest rotating globe.

Previous page, (clockwise from top): Beckett's Castle in Cape Elizabeth (*Courtesy of National Park Service*); Polar explorer Robert Peary, (*Courtesy of Wikicommons*); the Wedding Cake House in Kennebunkport (*Courtesy of Library of Congress*); a sign at the Percival Baxter Pet Cemetery on Mackworth Island in Falmouth (*From Author's Collection*).

Sounds of Sawmill First Heard in Old York

Along with being the birthplace of Maine author Sarah Orne Jewett, who wrote *The Country of the Pointed Firs*, Berwick is also the town where the first successful water-powered sawmill was built in North America.

Although some believe sawing operations began as early as 1623 in the wider area then known as York, the first well-documented water-powered sawmill was created in 1631 along the Great Falls River in South Berwick. In 1634, a model for a new mill and three carpenters arrived on the sailing ship *Pied Cow*, which also reportedly unloaded the first cattle in the new world. Cow Cove on the Salmon River, where they came ashore, is now part of Vaughan Woods Memorial State Park.

The 1634 mill, built by Ambrose Gibbens, and an associated gristmill were an immediate success. Within a few years the sawmill expanded to include nearly twenty saws. The mechanism was simple—just a water wheel connected to a long flat blade that moved up and down vertically.

Tall, straight white pine timbers were exported to England for use in navy vessels as masts and other components. The first multiple-gang sawmill was added in 1650.

The mill, as well as successive generations of other water-powered facilities, were located along the Great Forks River at today's Brattle Street Bridge. *Maine Atlas: M1, A3*

Real Pet Cemetery Honors Setters

Long before horror writer Stephen King made the concept of a pet cemetery really scary, one of Maine's foremost public figures created a special resting place for his beloved pets on Mackworth Island in Falmouth.

Percival Baxter, who would serve as Maine's governor between

1921 and 1925, and who stepped up to create Baxter State Park in Northern Maine, had his own pet cemetery with a view of Casco Bay from an island accessed via a causeway from the mainland.

It is the final resting place for fourteen of his beloved Irish setter dogs as well as one horse. Jerry Roan, a favorite horse of Baxter's, died at age thirty-five. His headstone notes he was a "noble horse and true friend."

When Garry Owen (Garry II), Baxter's constant companion in the State House died, the governor ordered the flags there to half-staff while the dog was being transported to Mackworth and laid to rest.

Unlike King's graveyard, there have been no reports of dead animals returning to life and terrorizing the countryside.

The island features a 1.4-mile public walking trail around its circumference. *Maine Atlas: M5, E5*

Castle Home to 'Friendly' Ghost

Considered by some as the state's most haunted house, Beckett's Castle, a private residence in Cape Elizabeth, is one of the most unusual homes in Maine.

Dominated by a thirty-foot tower with clocks in it, the two-thousand-square-foot residence was constructed of local gray fieldstone in the early 1870s. Prominent attorney, poet, and businessman Sylvester B.

Beckett designed the home for himself and personally built much of it. Beckett was a co-founder of the Portland Natural History Society, which eventually merged into Maine Audubon.

Among Beckett's contemporaries in the society was George Henry Preble, future admiral and son of Portland's renowned Commodore

Beckett's Castle, a private residence in Cape Elizabeth, is reportedly home to a "friendly" ghost. *Courtesy of National Park Service.*

Edward Preble and Alexander Dallas Bache, director of the US Geodetic Survey and great-grandson of Benjamin Franklin who did early survey work in Down East Maine.

Beckett reportedly held séances in the house and died there in 1882. His spirit supposedly appears from time to time as a glowing blue ball and is believed responsible for yanking blankets off beds and causing art to fall off the walls. After the property was restored, the ghost reportedly became more friendly.

When listed for sale in 2017, the three-bedroom house, which has been renovated and expanded, was listed for $3.35 million. *Maine Atlas: M3, A5*

Presidential Pull-Off Popular for Decades

It's rare when one stop lets you check off two Maine destinations at one time, but a popular pull-off along Ocean Avenue in Kennebunkport offers a trifecta.

For more than a century visitors have been drawn to that spot by two natural attractions, Blowing Cave and Spouting Rock. The cave operates much like Thunder Hole in Acadia, where the force of an incoming wave compresses air under a rock overhang, shooting the water back out and up with a ground-shaking thump.

Photographers have been trying to time the perfect shot of waves shooting skyward when hitting Spouting Rock for generations.

The spot is perhaps even more important today as it is also the site of a memorial constructed in 2009 honoring George H.W. Bush. It sports a bronze plaque and six-thousand-pound anchor and chain. The memorial, the perfect spot to see the Bush family house and compound on Walker's Point across the cove, honors the forty-first president as a friend of Kennebunkport and "An Anchor to Windward," a nautical reference to a safe place and prudent course of action. Bush and his wife, Barbara, were well-loved in the community and considered it their second hometown. *Maine Atlas: M3, D2*

The summer home of the late President George H.W. Bush and his wife, Barbara, in Kennebunkport. *Courtesy of Wikicommons.*

Island No 'Boon' for Marooned Crew

The crew of the *Nottingham Galley* must have thought they were in luck when they all made dry land after their vessel struck a submerged ledge at Boon Island six miles off York in the midst of a gale in early December 1710. Capt. John Deane and his thirteen crew members, however, quickly realized just how unlucky they were. Boon Island, which measures only thirty-three-feet by seven-hundred feet, is a treeless, windswept ledge devoid of food, shelter, or anything with which to make a fire. The cook soon died and his body was thrown into the sea. The ship's carpenter also soon perished.

The days stretched into weeks. With little more than mussels and the odd dead seabird for food, the crew reportedly resorted to cannibalism, eating the carpenter.

Finally, two men tried to reach shore in a makeshift raft. It broke apart and they drowned, but when their bodies washed ashore, people on the mainland decided to check on Boon Island and found the wretched survivors. The crew called their rescue after twenty-four days, "a boon from God," and so the island was named.

The first lighthouse on Boon Island was built of wood in 1799. The current stone tower, some 137 feet tall, was built in 1857 and remains the tallest in New England. *Maine Atlas: M1, B5*

Sebago Lake Holds Watery Graves

On May 16, 1944, just a few weeks before D-Day, a pair of British fighter pilots in training took off from the Brunswick Naval Air Station with two others for a routine training mission in their Vought F4U Corsairs. Among them were Sub-Lt. Vaughn Reginald Gill and Sub-Lt. Raymond Laurence Knott.

The flight headed to Sebago Lake to practice low-level flying over water. For some reason, the lead plane hit the lake and the plume of water and debris from the impact caused the second to go down.

Both planes quickly disappeared in more than two hundred feet of water of Maine's deepest lake. Both Gill and Knott were immediately listed as missing in action and declared dead later in the day.

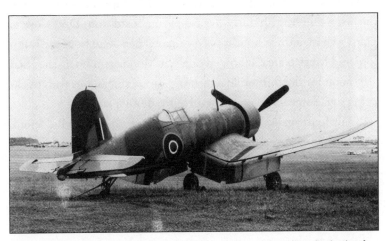

A pair of British Corsair aircraft, like the one pictured, crashed and sank into the depths of Sebago Lake in 1944. *Courtesy of Wikicommons.*

Despite an exhaustive search, the only sign of the pilots and aircraft found were an antenna and a headrest.

In 1998, Historic Aircraft Recovery Corporation conducted a side-scan sonar search of the lake bottom for the Corsairs and found wreckage that turned out to be a different WWII-era plane. In 2003, using a remote underwater vehicle, searchers found Knott's Corsair nose down on the bottom. Because even a damaged Corsair is worth hundreds of thousands of dollars, the company filed a salvage claim that was ultimately rejected by a judge after both the Maine and British governments objected. The wreckage of Gill's plane, believed to be about a mile away, has yet to be pinpointed.

In May 1944 a total of twenty-four aircraft accidents were logged at the Brunswick base. *Maine Atlas: M5, C1*

Cause of Excursion Disaster Remains Unknown

Exactly what happened aboard the ill-fated forty-four-foot excursion vessel *Don* when it sank somewhere in Casco Bay on June 29, 1941, may never be known. The *Don*, with Capt. Paul Johnson at the helm, set out with thirty-five people on board from Dyer Cove in Harpswell for a three-hour trip. Most passengers were from the Rumford and Mexico area. It arrived safely at Monhegan. It left later that afternoon for the forty-mile return trip on calm seas, but with thickening fog. Somewhere on the return trip disaster struck.

Only fourteen bodies were recovered from Harpswell to Biddeford. One of them was reportedly badly burned. None had been wearing life jackets. Among the bodies was that of Johnson who was found floating, tied to a small wooden barrel, wearing only undershorts.

The fact that watches on two of the bodies had both stopped at 11:40 suggests that whatever occurred happened fast, perhaps shortly before midnight.

Subsequent investigation revealed that the *Don* had sunk three times before and was overloaded on the fateful trip. When it left it was carrying 150 gallons of gasoline, including many large containers on deck.

The official inquiry ruled out an explosion and said most likely the top-heavy vessel tipped and sank either from sea conditions or striking an object. A memorial to the lost passengers was created in Mexico in 2008. The wreckage of the *Don* has never been found. *Maine Atlas: M6, D3*

Island was Arctic Hero's Home

Located just offshore in Harpswell, Eagle Island was once home to famed Arctic explorer Adm. Robert Peary. Peary is said to have been the first to reach the North Pole in 1909, his men equipped with sixty pairs of snowshoes hand-crafted by Mellie Dunham of Norway, Maine. Frederick Cook, a member of a decades-earlier Peary expedition, claimed he got to the North Pole a year earlier. Peary, however, was declared to be the first. Researchers in 1988 countered he had missed the mark by some sixty miles.

Peary bought Eagle Island in 1881 and began living there full-time in 1911. Peary, who was so busy being an explorer that he was home only for three years of the first twenty-three that he was married, died in 1920.

The wood-frame main house is protected from storm waves by a series of circular stone-walled rooms added by Peary in 1913. He housed his extensive collection of expedition artifacts in one of them.

Explorer Adm. Robert Peary, who lived on Eagle Island in Maine, in an early post-card view. *Author's collection.*

In 1967, his family donated the seventeen-acre island and home to the State of Maine, which now operates it as a park. A visitor's center was built in 2012. *Maine Atlas: M6, E2*

Cryptic Collection is One Of a Kind

Among the many quirky small private museums in the state, the International Cryptozoology Museum is without equal when it comes to paying homage to the weird, fanciful, and imagined—not just from Maine, but from around the world.

Cryptozoology, of course, is defined as the study of mythical and difficult to find creatures such as Sasquatch, the Loch Ness Monster and Mokele-mbembe. Such creatures are referred to in the aggregate as cryptids.

Located at 11 Avon Street on Thompson's Point in Portland, the museum, the only one in the world, is relatively easy to find, just look for the nine-foot statue of Bigfoot standing outside.

Inside you'll find purported samples of Yeti hair (from the Himalayan creature, not the expensive line of picnic coolers), lake monster exhibits, and displays covering the Dover Demon, the Montauk Monster, the Jersey Devil, Thylacine, Coelacanth, and the Napes/Skunk Ape, and more.

Props and oddities from movies, fanciful taxidermy creations, and all manner of scary-looking fictional reptiles abound.

The museum is the creation of Loren Coleman who opened it in 2003. After a series of moves and expansions it found its way to Thompson's Point. The museum is also affiliated with the International Cryptozoology Society formed in 2016. *Maine Atlas: M73, F2*

Old Gaol Maintained Law and Order

York may have been home to North America's first sawmill, but wood from that operation was required for more than just houses and

A full-size Bigfoot statue is the star attraction at the International Cryptozoology Museum in Portland, the only one of its kind in the world.
From Author's Collection. Used with permission.

ships stores. Records hint that the first jail in the community was built around 1656 although the earliest parts of the current "Old Gaol," weren't constructed until circa 1719. In frugal Maine fashion, some of the timbers from the first hoosegow, one of the first in North America, were recycled into the second.

The building, in which the town's Old York Historical Society (which operates several historic homes and museums in town) now keeps its treasures safe under lock and key, began as a simple stone jail cell with walls some two feet thick. Known as "the dungeon," it was expanded in 1736. Eventually the building came to include even more rooms for the jailer or warden and a second floor with additional cells.

You could be thrown in jail for not paying your bills in those days, but the good news was that the debtor's cell was a little larger, and nicer, than the general population—those miscreants incarcerated for crimes such as blasphemy, intoxication, and "idleness." Petty criminals were whipped or placed in the outdoor stocks. Serious criminals were hanged at Stage Neck.

It remained the county slammer until it was transferred to the town in 1760. It was used as a jail until 1879. The museum in the Old Gaol, located at the corner of Main and Lindsay streets, is open for tours seasonally. *Maine Atlas: M1, B5*

Freeport Desert No Down East Sahara

Riding up the highway into Maine in the 1960s, a kid couldn't help but be intrigued by a billboard sporting a giant camel and advertising "The Desert of Maine." Hmmm. A desert? In Maine?

Along with our trackless forests, high mountains, beaches, lakes, and rocky shores Maine also has a mini-desert, or at least forty acres of land in Freeport that bears a striking resemblance to one.

It seems a hapless farmer named Tuttle bought three hundred acres of the property back in 1797 unaware that just below the topsoil lay a deep layer of fine glacial silt. Over several generations, failure to rotate crops, overgrazing by sheep, and erosion resulted in the spreading of a bare patch and destruction of the land's fertility.

The Tuttles sold out to Henry Goldrup in 1919. He converted it into a tourist attraction in 1925.

Among the draws was Toona the camel. Another camel, Sarah, arrived in the 1950s. The facility now includes camel statues, a walking tour over the sparkling sands, an agricultural museum, the 223-year-old Tuttle barn, and a campground. Over the years the moving sands have enveloped a spring house that now lies buried under eight feet of sand.

The Desert of Maine is located, naturally, on Desert Road, just a few miles southwest of downtown's retail mecca. *Maine Atlas: M6, C1*

Globe is Largest on Earth

While most famous for its indispensable series of detailed atlases, including one for Maine, the former DeLorme Mapping Company literally shrunk the entire world down to manageable size when it built a its Yarmouth headquarters in 1998.

At 41.5-feet in diameter, Eartha is the largest rotating and revolving globe on the planet. Making a compete revolution every eighteen minutes, Eartha weighs just under three tons. More than six thousand pieces of aluminum form the globe's framework. It has the same twenty-three-degree tilt as the Earth. In 1999, it nudged out the previous record holder in Italy for the top spot in the *Guinness Book of World Records*.

Eartha was the brainchild of company founder David DeLorme and took two years to design and install. The 792 detailed photo-like sections that comprise the surface were made at a scale of sixteen miles to the inch. Technicians labored for more than a year to crunch 166 gigabytes of data to generate the imagery.

As major geographic events occur, such as the tsunami that

devastated Japan in 2011, panels are updated to more accurately reflect the situation on the ground.

Eartha is enclosed in a glass-walled, three-story lobby of the DeLorme Building at 2 DeLorme Drive, just off US Route 1 in Yarmouth. DeLorme was purchased by GPS company Garmin in 2016, but the lobby remains open to the public on weekdays. It is also visible through the windows.

In the Eartha lobby there's also a display about geocaching and a large collection of geocoins. *Maine Atlas: M6, D1*

Beachgoers Luck Out, See Lindy

Thousands of beachgoers in Old Orchard Beach today have no inkling that the sand under their blankets and umbrellas once formed a runway used by famed aviator Charles Lindberg.

While on a promotional tour following his record-setting transatlantic solo flight in 1927, Lindbergh was scheduled to stop at the Scarborough airports which served Portland at that time. Fog, however, prevented him being able to land there. After circling for more than an hour and a half, Lindbergh, unannounced, set the *Spirit of St. Louis* down on the beach in Old Orchard. Lucky Lindy was whisked off to his speaking engagement at the Eastland Hotel in Portland.

The beach was the town's official designated airport and was frequently used for auto racing as well. The *Spirit of St. Louis* was put into a hangar owned by Maine's most famous aviator, Harry Jones. Jones, who once landed his Wright biplane on Boston Common, made Maine's first airmail flight in 1919. Jones' hangar was destroyed by the Great Hurricane of 1938.

Lindbergh has other ties to Maine. The packing crate used to ship his plane back from France is now a private museum in Canaan. Anne Morrow, whom he married in 1929, spent many summers with her family on North Haven island in Penobscot Bay. The first woman to be licensed to fly gliders, she went on to be a successful author and set multiple flight records with her husband. *Maine Atlas: M3, B3*

Portsmouth Yard Actually in Kittery

Actually located in Kittery, the Portsmouth Naval Shipyard built the very first ship constructed for the fledgling US Navy. The USS *Raleigh* was built in 1776, although ships for the Royal Navy were built earlier. In an ironic twist, the USS *Raleigh* enjoyed a brief career before being driven aground. It was salvaged by the British and became the HMS *Raleigh*.

In 1885, the yard overhauled the USS *Constitution*. Also, the first submarine built by a US Navy yard and not a private company, was completed at Kittery. It was the *L8* which entered service in 1917. During World War II, the yard built some seventy submarines, including launching four in one day.

A prison built on the island eventually became known as "The Castle," due to its distinctive architecture. Over the years it held Spanish American War prisoners as well as captured German U-boat crews in addition to Navy and Marine inmates.

In 1905, a treaty ending the Sino-Russian War was signed at the yard following a lengthy peace conference. President Theodore Roosevelt won the Nobel Peace Prize for arranging it. The yard was named when the Navy believed the island was in New Hampshire waters. Over decades and numerous lawsuits, the Supreme Court ruled it is part of Kittery.

Nearly $340 million was budgeted in 2018 and 2019 for modernization work at the shipyard that employs more than seven thousand people. *Maine Atlas: M1, C4*

Ancient Curse Taints Saco's Waters

For years, even into the mid-twentieth century, some mothers throughout the valley of the Saco River would not let their children swim each summer until three people had drowned.

Their fears were based on a curse supposedly placed upon the river by a Native American sachem, Squandro, in revenge for the death of his infant son, Menewee, in 1675. The baby was reportedly taken from the arms of Squandro's wife near today's Factory Island and thrown into the river by three intoxicated European sailors who wanted to test a rumor that Native American babies could swim from birth. The child sank to the bottom and despite being rescued by his mother, died shortly afterwards.

Squandro, who for nearly fifty years had kept the peace in the area, cursed the river invoking that it take at least three non-native lives each year. He went on to encourage a band of warriors to attack coastal settlers in the first skirmish of King Phillips War.

Although scholars could find no record of the curse before 1880, for generations people believed the curse remained in force. In the late 1940s a year passed with no reported drownings. A *Maine Sunday Telegram* headline at the time announced "Saco River Outlives Curse of Indian Chief." *Maine Atlas: M71, B2*

Wonderful!

Famous House Looks Good Enough to Eat

Kennebunkport's Wedding Cake House has been impressing visitors for more than one hundred years. It was built in the Federal style in 1825 by local shipbuilder George W. Bourne, who later added a barn to the property. Like many New England homes, it developed in layers with a carriage house eventually connecting the house and barn.

The carriage house was demolished to save the main house when the barn caught fire in 1852. Bourne, perhaps inspired by the Gothic architecture he had seen on an earlier trip to Europe, rebuilt the barn and carriage house with five hand-crafted buttresses with pinnacles.

Not done yet, he continued stylizing the property by adding six buttresses and pinnacles to the house and then began adding more trim, right up until he died in 1856.

The entire structure, which has come to be called the Wedding Cake House, was restored in 1984. Located on Summer Street, it has earned the honor of being the most photographed house in Maine. *Maine Atlas: M3, D1*

Refusal to Remain Silent Saves Spring

Rachel Carson, a longtime visitor to Maine who built a summer house named "Silverledges" on the banks of the Sheepscot River on Southport Island, wrote the seminal book *Silent Spring*, a 1962 hit that warned of the dangers and hazards of pesticide use and abuse. The book opened with the words "It was a spring without voices. On the mornings that had once throbbed with the dawn chorus of robins, catbirds, doves, jays, wrens, and scores of other bird voices there was now no sound; only silence lay over the fields and woods and marsh."

Biologist and author Rachel Carson.
Courtesy of Digicommons.

The book rocked the chemical industry and resulted in the banning of DDT, which was killing

The ornate Wedding Cake House in Kennebunkport.
Courtesy of Library of Congress.

birds and other animals all over the country. DDT was involved in reproductive failures that almost spelled extinction for American bald eagles and peregrine falcons.

Carson, a biologist and author, died in 1964. She was posthumously awarded the Presidential Medal of Freedom in 1980.

Memorials to Carson's pioneering book, and her work as editor and chief of US Fish and Wildlife publications, include The Rachel Carson National Wildlife Reserve along the coast from Wells to Cape Elizabeth, The Rachel Carson Salt Pond Preserve in New Harbor, and greenways in Maine and Maryland. *Maine Atlas: M1, B5*

Tower a Reminder of Castle's Glory

Far from a place for lords and ladies, and not even built of stone, the Casco Castle in South Freeport dominated the imagination at the turn of twentieth century.

It was not developed as a private home, but rather an attraction to increase passenger traffic on the Brunswick-Yarmouth Street Railway, a trolley line owned by Amos Gerald. He built the first trolley line in Maine as well as the first electrical generating plant.

Except for a single stone tower that now remains on private property, the Castle was actually a hotel constructed of wood in 1903. Gray shingles simulated stone giving it an appearance of permanence from a distance. Stairs led to the top of

The Casco Castle looms near the shore in Freeport in this old postcard view. *Author's collection.*

its main stone tower, which was nearly one-hundred-feet high. A draw-bridge was added later. There were formal gardens, as well as rooms for one hundred guests. A surrounding park was open to the public as was a small zoo. The associated Castle Ballpark was an instant hit.

The glow lasted only a few years, however. The Castle burned to the ground in the fall of 1914 with flames shooting from the tower. The best place to see the remaining tower is from Winslow Park on Winslow Park Way. *Maine Atlas: M6, D1*

Umbrella Cover Collection Sparks World Record

Looking for something far from ordinary to do on a rainy day? Especially if it's pouring cats and dogs? Consider taking a ferry ride to the Umbrella Cover Museum on Peaks Island off Portland. Founder Nancy Hoffman proudly proclaims the institution is dedicated to "the appreciation of the mundane in everyday life." What's not to like?

Hoffman started back in 1996 with a collection of six different cloth covers. Naturally, that inspired her to open a museum—started in the kitchen of her home. In 2002, it moved to the current location at 62-B Island Avenue.

By 2012, the collection had grown to more than 730 covers, which won her a place in the *Guinness Book of World Records*.

Since then, it has mushroomed; Hoffman reported in January 2020 that the museum had more than two thousand different umbrella covers from more than sixty-nine countries. Exhibits change and each cover has its own story. Records are kept on the origin and provenance of each.

The museum is open from Memorial Day to Labor Day. It doesn't hurt to contact her via the info on the museum website to confirm hours. Oh, and don't forget to pack your umbrella! *Maine Atlas: M3, A5*

The Grave of a Not-So-Wicked Witch

The legends surrounding the grave of Mary Nasson in the Old Burying Yard in York Village have swung far and wide over the decades, with most focusing on a belief she was a witch. However, there's plenty of evidence that isn't so, despite the colorful reasons given for that superstition.

Some believe it was the carved figure of a woman with wide-open eyes, ample bosom, and a large mound of hair on the distinctive headstone that got it started. Others claim the long, heavy slab of stone covering the grave was there to keep her from arising to do evil from beyond the grave.

Mary Nasson's likeness reaches out from her headstone in the Old Burying Yard in York Village.
Courtesy of Digicommons.

Most likely, many graves of that era had such capstones which prevented animals from disturbing the remains. And, it is unlikely Mary, who died at age 29 in 1774, would have been given a Christian burial if deemed a witch. Plus, the Salem Witch Trials happened decades earlier. She may have been an herbalist and healer. People still leave coins on the grave as a sort of offering. *Maine Atlas: M1, B5*

One of dozens of distinctive outdoor works of art in the Outdoor Sculpture Garden at the Ogunquit Museum of American Art.
Courtesy of Library of Congress.

Sun Also Rises on Sculpture Garden

Spread across three acres of ocean-side grounds at the Ogunquit Museum of American Art, the Outdoor Sculpture Garden displays a wide range of pieces by some of the nation's top contemporary artists. They are set within an attractive sylvan setting that features flower beds, a reflecting pool, shady groves, and secluded benches. Works by Langlais, Dirks, Fitzhugh, Schultze, and Greenbaum are featured there.

The museum was a dream fulfilled by its founder, Henry Strater, an artist who first came to Ogunquit in 1919 and painted in Paris between the world wars. A friend and fishing buddy to Ernest Hemingway, and inspiration for a character in an F. Scott Fitzgerald novel, Strater moved to Maine permanently in 1925.

Ogunquit had long been a magnet to artists and an Art Colony Walking Tour of the Perkins Cove area begins at the museum. Opened in 1956, the museum is the only one in Maine dedicated solely to American art. It houses more than three thousand paintings, prints, drawings, sculptures, photographs, and other items and has hosted exhibitions of works by Rockwell Kent, Marsden Hartley, Dahlov Ipcar, Andrew Wyeth, Jamie Wyeth, and Edward Hopper.

The museum and garden, which is open daily from May 1 through October 31, is located overlooking Narrow Cove at 543 Shore Road in Ogunquit. There are photography restrictions. *Maine Atlas: M1, A5*

Fanciful Signs Point the Way

Maine's World Traveler Signpost in Lynchville near Bethel may be the most famous, and original, of the must-see novelties in the state. But it is far from the only one. Three other signs are sprinkled around the state and really should be counted if you want to collect a photograph of yourself with all of them.

With extra points for originality, the Presidential Signpost in Casco points the way to communities with names similar to past presidents including Washington, Jefferson, Madison, Monroe, Jackson, (Take that White Mountains), Van Buren, Harrison, Lincoln, Garfield Plantation, and Clinton.

That doesn't mean all those towns were actually named for our chief executives. Jackson was named for Revolutionary War General Henry Jackson. Harrison was named for an early landowner. Lincoln took that name in 1829, long before Abe's appearance, when the town decided to ditch the name Mattanawcook. Clinton was named for New York Gov. DeWitt Clinton.

The presidential sign post is located across from the Village Green at the corner of Route 121 and Leach Hill Road. *Maine Atlas: M5, A1*

There's another popular signpost that also sports the names of towns in Maine with international counterparts, but in a different order. It can be found in South China at the intersection of Jones Road and Village Street, on the northwest corner. *Maine Atlas: M13, B3*

A third international places sign can be found in Norway. It sports the names of towns in Maine that have corresponding communities in other countries overseas. It is located in the parking lot of The Lake Store on Route 118. *Maine Atlas: M11, D1*

Tower Reminder of Town's Legacy

Although it was once part of a much larger preserve, the vintage water tower in Saco's Pepperell Park is a stalwart reminder of the city's proud past.

A donation of $10,000 from Cornelius Sweetser allowed the development of the park on land donated by the family of the town's founder,

A vintage postcard view of Pepperell Park in Saco showing its distinctive tower in the distance. *Author's collection.*

Sir William Pepperell, a hero of the Battle of Louisbourg during King George's War. In fact, the town originally was named Pepperellborough, but after folks decided it was too difficult to spell, they voted to change it to Saco in 1805.

In the early years, the park included a cemetery, fountain, picnic areas, land for a church, and a trotting park. The eighteen-foot-tall stone water tower, designed by Horace Wadlin in 1887, provided water to care for the surrounding grounds. Capable of storing around 7,600 gallons of water, it sits atop an abandoned well some 250 feet deep.

In 1893, the Legislature gave Saco the option of moving the graves or undertaking actions "to arrange that part of said park where said bodies now are, as may be deemed consistent and in harmony with the other arrangements of said park." A memorial stone close to the water tower on School Street lists the names of those originally interred in the graveyard.

The town built the Gov. John Fairfield Elementary School in the middle of the original park in the 1960s. *Maine Atlas: M71, B3*

L.L.Bean

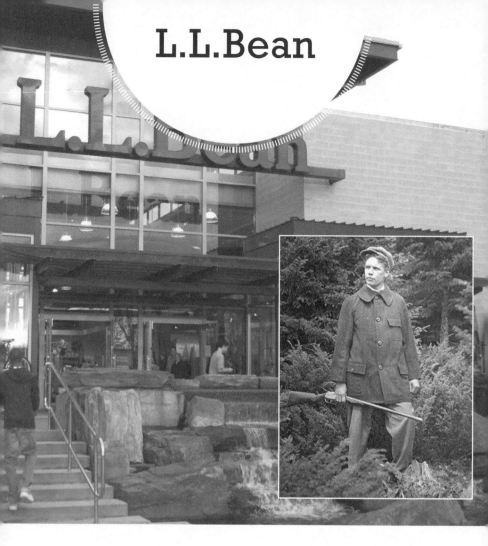

L.L.Bean was founded in 1912 by Leon Leonwood Bean of Freeport who invented his signature rubber-bottom, leather-top hunting shoes after returning from hunting with cold and wet feet. Within a year, and after perfecting the design, he was selling them to other avid sportsmen. His mail-order business, and later the retail store, flourished.

An insistence on quality, and the best guarantee around, helped fuel rapid growth. Since 1951, the flagship Freeport store has remained open twenty-four-hours a day, year-round. In fact, there are no locks on the doors. It has only closed a handful of times, each for a few hours, including once to allow workers to attend L.L.'s funeral.

Its Own Zip Code

The company's mail-order operation in Freeport is so massive it had the distinction of having its own Zip Code (04033) assigned in 1976.

Giant Maine Hunting Shoe

The giant Maine hunting shoe outside the entrance to the flagship store in Freeport is a popular selfie and photo location. It stands sixteen feet high and is reportedly the equivalent of a size 410 shoe.

Bootmobile

Created to celebrate the company's one hundredth anniversary in 2012, L.L.Bean's "Bootmobile" roams the Northeast, often appearing in parades, promoting the company, and sharing information on its products. Built on a Ford 250 pickup truck frame, the twenty-foot long steel and fiberglass boot stands thirteen feet tall. The laces are braided nautical rope capable of holding 100,000 pounds.

Moose Locked in Combat

Visible from both inside and outside of the flagship store, the largest taxidermy display in Maine features a pair of bull moose that died after their antlers became locked while battling during the rut in Northern Maine in 2005. It was crafted by Mark Dufresne of Nature's Reflections Taxidermy in Gray. The title of the display is "The Final Charge."

Riverbed Aquarium

When the flagship store was remodeled in 1984, a trout pond holding live fish was created in the center. The store added a 3,500-gallon "Riverbed Aquarium" in 2007. It features acrylic domes on the bottom where as many as a million visitors each year can go up inside the display to see live fish swimming in the current.

The main entrance to the L.L.Bean flagship retail store in Freeport. Until the coronavirus in 2020 it had only closed for a few hours on a couple occasions to allow employees to attend funerals. *(From Author's Collection)*. Inset: A young Leon Leonwood Bean. *Courtesy of Digicommons.*

Portland

Maine's largest city has risen from the ashes more than once in a proud history that dates back 11,000 years to the peninsula's occupation by Native Americans. They called the place Machigonne.

The first Europeans arrived in 1632 and named their settlement Casco. The name was later changed to Falmouth and eventually to Portland. This island-studded, natural harbor is the closest major port in the United States to Europe.

The first settlements were raided and burned by Native Americans multiple times in the late 1600s, and the town was bombarded and burned by the British during the American Revolution. During the Civil War in 1863, Portland residents managed to fend off a raid by the Confederate Navy.

In 1866, a devastating fire swept through the town destroying 1,800 buildings. More than 10,000 people were left homeless.

Still, Portland has managed to return after each calamity stronger and better than ever. It served as the state's first capital and remains its largest center of community, commerce, and culture. *Maine Atlas: M73, E3-4, and F3-4*

Monument to the First Settlers

Located on the Eastern Promenade, Portland's first public monument, erected in 1883, honors George Cleeves and Richard Tucker who are believed to the city's first settlers. They moved from across the bay in 1632. The sides of the obelisk are engraved with all four historic names for the city.

British Attack

In October 1775, while the British occupied Boston, a fleet under command of Capt. Henry Mowat attacked Falmouth. After giving people two hours to evacuate, cannons unloaded incendiary shot. Landing parties continued the destruction until, according to Mowat,

Opposite (clockwise from top): The USS Constitution (*Courtesy of Library of Congress*): More than 600 structures were destroyed when a great fire destroyed much of Portland on July 4, 1866 (*Courtesy of Digicommons*); The statue of native son Henry Wadsworth Longfellow in Longfellow Square in Portland (*Courtesy of Library of Congress*).

"the body of the town was in one flame." More than four hundred buildings were destroyed.

USS *Constitution*

During a visit to Portland in 1931, *Old Ironsides*, which sports masts made from trees felled in Unity, Maine, was the talk of the town. According to historian Herb Adams, Frederick Hall, a US senator from Maine, proposed moving the ship's homeport to Portland during a reception for the crew. Although the idea received widespread acclaim, it never came to fruition.

Edward Preble, who watched the British burn his hometown of Falmouth in 1775, became the USS *Constitution's* commodore in 1803. The vessel's last commander under sail when it made that visit to Maine was Commander Louis Gulliver of Portland.

Longfellow House

The house and garden on Congress Street where poet Henry Wadsworth Longfellow grew up was the first house museum established in Maine. It is now run by the Maine Historical Society. Among Longfellow's most famous works are "Paul Revere's Ride," "Evangeline: A Tale of Acadie," and "The Rainy Day."

Kotzschmar Organ

When Cyrus Curtis gave the mansion-size Kotzschmar Memorial Organ to the City of Portland in 1911, it was the second largest organ in the world. Located in the Merrill Auditorium on Myrtle Street, and lovingly restored in 2014, the organ features five keyboards, 330 keys, and more than seven thousand pipes.

Maine's First Capital

When Maine split from Massachusetts to become its own state in 1820, Portland served as its first capital, holding that designation until 1832. The first State House, a brick building, was located at the corner of Congress and Myrtle streets. It burned in the Great Fire of 1866.

The Birthplace of Chewing Gum

John Bacon Curtis created the country's first large-scale chewing gum factory at 291 Fore Street (now Hub Furniture) in Portland in 1866. His concoction involved adding wax and sugar to spruce gum, that insidious, sticky substance found on the bark of spruce trees. Other flavors were eventually added.

Portland Observatory

Built in 1807 by Capt. Lemuel Moody on Munjoy Hill, the Portland Observatory used flags to alert ship owners of the arrival of their vessels. It stands eight-six feet high and remained in use until the advent of two-way radios. Greater Portland Landmarks took over care of the wooden structure in 1984. Tours are offered daily in season.

Portland's Great Fire

On July 4, 1866, a fire started by a firecracker or flick of a cigar ash, near the city docks, spread northward, fanned by strong winds. It swept through the city center destroying City Hall, the Customs House, the Post Office, banks, churches, hotels, and offices. It was the largest municipal conflagration in the United States to that date. The federal government sent 1,500 tents to help house those who lost their homes. Within four months, more than six hundred structures had been rebuilt.

Getting on Track in Maine

The history of Maine railroading goes back almost all the way to the state's beginnings. The first operating line was the Bangor and Piscataquis, which opened between the Queen City and Old Town in 1836. Scores of smaller lines eventually consolidated into the big three including Maine Central, Boston and Maine, and Bangor and Aroostook. Not wanting to be left out of the railroad gold rush in the late 1800s, numerous smaller companies formed to serve rural and backcountry areas. Because of Maine's rugged terrain, and the expense of materials and laying track, many early railroads adopted a track gauge of two feet when standard gauge was four feet, eight and a half inches.

Some of these "short" lines served single industries including the Monson railroad which hauled slate from quarries. It was known as the "Old Two by Six," in reference to its track gauge and the length of its main line in miles.

The busiest line in Maine today is the Canadian Pacific which runs from Holeb in the west to Vanceboro in the east.

The heyday of Maine railroading was in 1924 when there were 2,380 active miles of track. Many of those lines over the years have been converted to recreational trails.

Gulf Stream Trestle

Gulf Stream Trestle in Bingham allowed the Somerset Railroad to carry visitors from the southern part of the state to a station at Rockwood, on Moosehead Lake, across from the Kineo Resort. The 700-foot-long steel bridge, the second tallest ever built in Maine at 115 feet high, was constructed in 1904. It was abandoned in 1933 and torn down in 1976. *Maine Atlas: M30, C4*

An early postcard view of Gulf Stream Trestle in Bingham on the Somerset Railroad. *Author's collection.*

Down East Scenic Railway

From its terminus in Washington Junction in Ellsworth, the Down East Scenic Railway provides excursion trains over tracks that once were traveled by the historic Bar Harbor Express, which brought scores of summer residents from Philadelphia and New York to Maine. The ninety-minute trips on the train, which include an open-air car and vintage passenger coaches, cover more than thirteen miles, over which eagles, ospreys, and other wildlife can be seen. *Maine Atlas: M24, E2*

Sandy River and Rangeley Lakes Railroad

This narrow gauge historical railroad is lovingly operated on weekends by volunteers offering trips using vintage equipment that once was used to connect towns and villages in the Rangeley Lakes Region. The short excursions begin in Phillips at an authentic depot and include a small railroad yard where passengers can explore a turntable, shops, and other equipment. *Maine Atlas: M19, B3*

Wiscasset, Waterville, and Farmington Railway Museum

Never actually making it all the way to the last two towns in its name, this narrow gauge operation is preserved by volunteers running over nearly three miles of track. Regular trips are made in season from the museum and Sheepscot Depot in Alna using a vintage steam locomotive. Equipment from other Maine narrow gauge lines, including the Bridgton and Saco and Monson railroads, are on display. *Maine Atlas: M7, A2*

Maine Narrow Gauge Railroad and Museum

Running on 1.5 miles of waterfront track along Casco Bay at the Eastern Promenade in Portland, trains operated by the Maine Narrow Gauge Railroad include both open and enclosed cars pulled by a mix of steam and diesel locomotives. Exhibits include rolling stock and other related items. From Thanksgiving to Christmas the museum operates a special Polar Express train featuring an appearance by Santa. *Maine Atlas: M73, E4*

Boothbay Railway Village

Located on Route 27, the Boothbay Railway Village features a sprawling historic village, and trips on an actual three-quarter-mile narrow-gauge railroad that operates from a depot moved from Freeport. There is also a forty-foot-by-twenty-six-foot model railroad and more. An antique automobile exhibit is also part of the facility. *Maine Atlas: M7, C2*

Onawa Trestle, Maine's tallest, crosses the outlet of Lake Onawa.
Borestone Mountain is in the distance.
Courtesy of Eric Sturgeon.

Onawa Wreck

Maine's worst railroad disaster occurred on December 20, 1919 on the Canadian Pacific Line near the tiny outpost of Onawa, just east of Monson. Due to a dispatching error, a freight train collided head-on with an eleven-coach passenger train carrying immigrants who had just arrived in North America. A total of twenty-three people died and fifty more were seriously injured. *Maine Atlas: M41, E5*

Belfast and Moosehead Lake Railroad

Like most of Maine's coastal startup railroads, the Belfast and Moosehead Lake Railroad never made it very far inland, eventually only reaching about thirty-five miles to Burnham Junction. Although it stopped operations in 2007, the railway remains alive today under the nonprofit Brooks Preservation Society with a robust excursion schedule including rides in the summer and fall seasons, charters and special holiday Santa Express trains.

Maine's hardy river drivers, depicted on an early postcard, kept saw logs and pulp flowing to mills downriver.
Author's collection.

Acknowledgments

Developing a list of people, places, things, and events that are pivotal to understanding Maine didn't happen in a vacuum. The ideas filtered in over time, in conversations with people from Kittery to Fort Kent, notes made while on road trips and back country excursions for more than a decade, and emails sent to myself after seeing a clue somewhere else and promising to circle back and learn more.

To produce *Wild! Weird! Wonderful! Maine*, more than 550 items were ultimately nominated for inclusion, although the realities of space, time, and expense ultimately required that list be reduced to around three hundred. Naturally, not everyone would assign the same priorities and if your favorite story of Maine, or quirky personality or place didn't make the cut, please don't be insulted. If you are, my apologies. All I can say is don't hesitate to send along your suggestions because there's always a chance for a sequel.

Once the list was finalized, research and rounding up images began. There's no way that any one person could possibly get all the needed images alone and, in fact, even ten years ago, before the advent of digital commons and voluminous online photo libraries, it would probably be impossible. Fortunately, friends made over a nearly forty-year career in local journalism, and folks I've met over decades of adventures helped me out. The list of those who have gone the extra mile to help, loaning images, taking photos, getting permission to use others, and verifying facts appears below. Thank you all. You are true generous spirits of Maine.

In no particular order they include: Tessie Dubois, Rachel Rice, David Allen, Tina Radel, Chief Janine Roberts, Mark Putnam, Dot Roberts, Kevin Burnham, Joe LaChance, Paul Merrill, David Cookson, Tony Levesque, Nathaniel Boechat, Paul Cyr, Alain Ouellette, Steve Cartwright, Natalie Liberace, Scott Monroe, Todd Benoit,

Kathy Upton, Mark Messer, Patricia Lane, Barbara Saunders, Charles Leighton, Julie Brownie, Steve Fontaine, Jim Murton, Stephen Hussar, Edward French, Kate Steed, Kim Smith, Timothy Hobbs, Dan Bookham, Bill Pierce, Liz Graves, Cathie Pelletier, Jeff Nichols, Elaine Jones, Kate O'Brien, Peter Roberts, Harry Gordon, James Bennett, Ron Beard, Louis Pelletier, Steve Young, Kelly Ryder, Melanie Brooks, Ron Chase, Matt Sawyer, Eric Sturgeon, Larry B. Bonney, Nancy Marshall, Chip Carey, Loren Coleman, Laura Snyder Smith, Don Carrigan, Letitia Baldwin, Hugh French, Sandi Day, Heidi Murphy, Lois Ann Gordon, Karen Raye, Howard Hutchins, Steve Fountain, Robert Skoglund, Holly Anderson, Deborah McDermott, Bob Godfrey, Scott Riddell, Kevin Bennett, Trudy Wyman, Wanda Wilcock, Al Cowperthwaite, Mark Mogensen, H. Joie Crockett, Rachel Wilkenson, Jenn Pye, Ulrike Welsch, Nancy Hoffman, Jack Russell and Laura Chaney.

Of course, there would not be a *Wild! Weird! Wonderful! Maine*, if publisher Dean Lunt wasn't willing to take on the project. Islandport Press, more than any other publisher in the state, really "gets" Maine and understands the importance of keeping timeless classics available as well as fielding an ambitious annual list of new titles. And thanks too to Teresa Lagrange who turned files containing more than 2,500 raw images into this book's wonderful design.

About the Author

Earl Brechlin, a longtime Maine journalist, has written several non-fiction books featuring Maine, including hiking guides and *Forever Yours, Bar Harbor*, a book of antique postcard images. After graduating from the University of Maine, Brechlin moved to Mount Desert Island where he worked as an island gardener. After first taking a job in the print shop, he soon rose to serve as editor of *The Bar Harbor Times* for nearly twenty years and was then founding editor of the *Mount Desert Islander* in 2001. Brechlin, now communications director for Friends of Acadia, is also a registered Maine Guide, a model railroad enthusiast, and sometimes attends comic book conventions to tout his Ancient Alien Expert business, offering interested parties potential degrees in Ancient Astronaut Theory, Cryptozoology, Zombie Survival, and Middle Earth History. He lives in Bar Harbor with his wife, Roxie, a retired kindergarten teacher.